Praise for *Smart Leadership*

"*Smart Leadership* is packed with wisdom and practicality, seasoned with real-world experience. Leaders who want to be more effective, add more value, and scale their impact now have the guide they have been searching for. Read this book, make these simple, smart choices and take your leadership to the next level."

—Jon Gordon, best-selling author of *The Power of Positive Leadership*

"If you want to be a great leader, then you must read *Smart Leadership*. It's a playbook on how to make four simple choices to scale and grow your impact as a leader . . . Mark Miller combines his decades of leadership experience, well-documented research, and pragmatic steps to get you on your way to leadership excellence."

—Charlene Li, *New York Times* bestselling author and Founder of Altimeter

"Increasing your impact can feel like a complex and confusing process—no matter the industry or job. Miller has written the ultimate guide to leading intentionally and creating spaces to impact your team and company in the most meaningful ways. *Smart Leadership* provides a thoughtful and powerful new approach to leadership."

—Marshall Goldsmith is the New York Times #1 bestselling author of *Triggers, Mojo, and What Got You Here Won't Get You There*

"The four choices Mark outlines are as powerful and lifechanging as they are pragmatic. He shows all of us how to exercise our own superpower to scale our impact. Mark proves once again he's a rock star who not only inspires but gives practical tools anyone can follow."

—Emily Thomas Kendrick, CEO of Arrow Exterminators

"Mark Miller is one of the smartest leaders I know, and he's researched some of the best leaders and companies of the last century. I'm grateful he's condensed his learnings that are usually reserved for one giant chicken sandwich company and finally made it available to all of us. Too many leaders are trying to work harder instead of smarter. This book will give you the tools to reverse that in your life and with your teams."

—Jason Jaggard, Founding Partner of Novus Global and Cofounder of the Meta Performance™ Institute

"Whether you are leading yourself or a team of hundreds, Smart Leadership is a must read; an 'extra highlighter required' kind of leadership book. Mark Miller challenges the reader to take a hard look at their personal and/or professional quicksand, nudging towards a reality that is both inspirational and scary—and that's just the beginning . . . *Smart Leadership* is filled with creative best practices, actionable take-aways and the very best of story-telling."

—**Jennifer Goodwyn, President & COO of Snellings-Walters**

"Books by Mark Miller are valuable for anyone with an honest desire to grow as a leader. But I feel that THIS is the book I've waited for more than 20 years for him to write. As you turn these pages, you'll discover a carefully curated collection of Mark's profound insights and practical teaching. It's all woven together with his straightforward wisdom—pieced together from decades of personal growth, research, humbling difficulties, and best-in-class experience . . . I know Mark has more to teach us than one book could contain, but this comes mighty close to having him as your personal mentor."

—**Zack Clark, Founder and Lead Spokesman of Development & Leadership Coaching**

"Mark's book is packed with information that impacts. The relatable and immediately applicable material makes it a fast and enjoyable read."

—**Dave Anderson, President, Learn To Lead**

"I've always felt the key to lasting change is to pick a few high-impact actions and do them well and in the right sequence. In a time of chaos and disruption it's the only way to stay focused and on track. That's why I like Mark Miller's book. He zeroes in on four choices that help us start digging out of the quicksand that drags us down (and burns us out) and start growing into influential leaders."

—**Quint Studer, Author of** *Wall Street Journal* **bestseller** *The Busy Leader's Handbook: How to Lead People and Places That Thrive*

SMART
LEADERSHIP

ALSO BY MARK MILLER

THE HIGH PERFORMANCE SERIES

Chess Not Checkers
Leaders Made Here
Talent Magnet
Win the Heart
Win Every Day

OTHER BOOKS

The Heart of Leadership
The Secret of Teams
*Great Leaders Grow**
*The Secret**

ADDITIONAL RESOURCES

Smart Leadership in Action Journal
*Smart Leadership Field Guide***
*Chess Not Checkers Field Guide***
*Talent Magnet Field Guide***
*Win the Heart Field Guide***
*Win Every Day Field Guide***
*The Secret Field Guide***
The Heart of Leadership Field Guide
The Secret of Teams Field Guide

* Coauthored with Ken Blanchard
** Coauthored with Randy Gravitt

SMART
LEADERSHIP

Four Simple

Choices to Scale

Your Impact

MARK MILLER

Matt Holt Books
An Imprint of BenBella Books, Inc.
Dallas, TX

BenBella Books, Inc.
10440 N. Central Expressway
Suite 800
Dallas, TX 75231
benbellabooks.com
Send feedback to feedback@benbellabooks.com

BenBella is a federally registered trademark.
Matt Holt and logo are trademarks of BenBella Books.

Printed in the United States of America
10 9 8 7 6 5 4 3 2 1

Library of Congress Control Number: 2021034772
ISBN TK 9781953295750
eISBN TK 9781637740095

Editing by Katie Dickman
Copyediting by Ginny Glass
Proofreading by Sarah Vostok and Jenny Bridges
Indexing by Amy Murphy
Text design and composition by PerfecType, Nashville, TN
Cover design by Brigid Pearson
Author photo by Mary Caroline Russell
Printed by Lake Book Manufacturing

To Jimmy Collins: Thanks for showing me, and countless others, what a Smart Leader looks like. And thanks for introducing me to the work of Peter Drucker!

CONTENTS

Introduction 1

SCALE YOUR IMPACT

Swimming in Quicksand 8

Your Real Superpower 21

SMART CHOICE #1
CONFRONT REALITY

Confront Reality 36

Check the Mirror 58

Review Your Crew 72

SMART CHOICE #2
GROW CAPACITY

Grow Capacity 88

Stop and Think 106

Expand Your Energy 120

SMART CHOICE #3
FUEL CURIOSITY

Fuel Curiosity 136

Ask, Don't Tell 156

Talk with Strangers 172

SMART CHOICE #4
CREATE CHANGE

Create Change 186

See the Unseen 202

Sharpen Your Tools 216

Be Smart! 231

Acknowledgments 235

Additional Resources 239

Notes 241

Index 247

INTRODUCTION

I n the movie *Indiana Jones and the Last Crusade*, one of the most oft-quoted lines comes from the climactic scene. If you saw the film, you remember the moment.

Indiana Jones, under extreme duress, has found the hidden chamber containing the Holy Grail, the cup of Christ from the Last Supper. As legend has it, anyone who drinks from the cup will never die.

Now, the final challenge remaining for Indy is to select the correct cup from among the many on display. Ironically, based on outward appearance, the imposters all looked "better" than the real chalice. As Indy surveys the situation, he is joined by the villain, who also wants the cup. Having no apparent alternative, our hero relinquishes the choice to the bad guy.

Confronted with the many options before him, the antagonist chooses a beautiful gold cup inlaid with precious stones. After drinking from it, he experiences a gruesome and painful death in a matter of seconds. The knight who has been faithfully guarding the cup for seven centuries utters the now famous line: "He chose ... poorly."

Indy, driven by different decision criteria, points to a simple, more ordinary cup. "That's the cup of a carpenter."

The knight concurs, "You have chosen wisely."

As leaders, most of us are not chasing immortality, but we do want to make a difference. What's holding us back from accomplishing all we have envisioned? There could be several culprits: you may still be developing the fundamental skills required to lead well, or perhaps you have not yet become the type of leader people want to follow. The latter is an issue of leadership character. Although both are possibilities, they are not the focus of this book.

Assuming you have the character and skills to lead, there is one more crucial ingredient required for you to reach your full potential: your choices. This book is dedicated to this simple truth:

Your choices determine your impact.

Why is it so difficult to make wise choices? The problem is multifaceted—the pace of change, uncertainty in our world, competing priorities, shrinking resources, increasing demands, staggering levels of complexity, and more. All of these factors appear to be conspiring against leaders who are committed to creating positive change. Many leaders seem to be swimming in quicksand. The most frustrating part is that the harder they work, the deeper they sink. A leader's choices, however, can be his or her lifeline.

Have you ever considered the real, tangible impact of your choices? Our poor choices may not result in an instantaneous mortal meltdown as Dr. Jones observed, but the consequences are all around us—the morale of those we lead, their level of engagement, the culture we've created or allowed to exist, the reputation we've earned in the marketplace, the brand loyalty we have or have not built, the sales, profits, and customer reports are all a direct reflection of our choices. Although this may be a sobering list, the actual list of what's at stake is much longer and even more personal, including your health, your family, and your legacy.

Anyone who has led anything knows that leaders make countless choices. How do we look past the next new shiny object, the mounting pressure to perform, and competing priorities to maximize our leadership impact? It's about our choices. Our choices literally have the power to change our world.

As you know, not all choices have equal value. This truth begs several questions: What are the choices that matter most? Which choices have the greatest strategic value? Which choices enable other choices? If you want the answers to these questions and more, please keep reading.

I started writing this book decades ago. I just didn't know it. As a young leader, I stumbled and bumbled along with a deep sense that I could be more effective, add more value, and have greater impact. I just didn't know how.

Then I read *The Effective Executive* by Peter Drucker. If you haven't read it, put this book down and go buy it. Although Drucker wrote his classic more than fifty years ago, much of the content is still spot-on today. I remember being intrigued by his statement:

Effectiveness can be learned. Effectiveness must be learned.

So wait. Is this a book on effectiveness or adding value or creating more impact? Yes. All of the above. Effectiveness is a lifelong quest to add more value. When you and I add more value to the organizations we serve, we generate more impact. It's impossible to have more impact without becoming more effective. But never confuse the strategy with the goal—effectiveness is the strategy; the goal is impact.

HOW THIS BOOK IS ORGANIZED

In the opening pages, we will calibrate the magnitude of the challenges you and other leaders are facing. Often, we need to name a thing before we can conquer it. We'll survey the quagmire, but we'll not linger there—you are likely all too familiar with it. My intent is to stir in you a renewed desire to escape the daily challenges that are limiting your impact and eroding your quality of life. Some of you have tried but have become so exhausted and frustrated, it may have been a while since you last attempted to extricate yourself.

I also want to use these early pages to remind you why our choices matter so much. In short, they give us agency, accountability, opportunity, and true power. For most of you, this will serve only as a reminder, but a very important reminder nonetheless.

The balance of the book is organized around the four Smart Choices. After an introductory chapter on each choice, you'll find two chapters, each devoted to what I call a best practice. These chapters are intended to help you activate your Smart Choice.

These supporting chapters contain strategies and tactics that work. However, they are not intended to create a checklist. There are countless ways to operationalize each of the Smart Choices. My intent is to provide you with a proven place to start. All choices of consequence begin in the head but must move to your hands.

I'm sure some of the best practices outlined in the following pages will not resonate with you or feel applicable in your situation. That's okay. Perhaps they will stimulate your thinking as you create your own list of tactics. The value of the choice is only realized in the practices it generates.

At the end of each chapter, you will see a short paragraph entitled "Be Smart!" The intent is to give you one or two ideas for immediate action—ways to move the choice from your head to your hands. I hope you'll find value in these suggestions.

THE PROMISE OF THIS BOOK

For the last twenty years, my team and I have been talking to leaders. We have interviewed hundreds of them. These women and men represent some of the best organizations in the world, including Apple, Southwest Airlines, Google, the Navy SEALs, Zappos, Starbucks,

FedEx, the Mayo Clinic, Disney, Clemson football, Cirque du Soleil, and many more.

In addition to this qualitative work, we have surveyed thousands of leaders and individual contributors, invested untold hours on desk research, and conducted multiple in-field validation studies with real leaders, their employees, and their customers.

We collected a mountain of data, actions, priorities, habits, and disciplines from leaders around the world; we also heard about successes, failures, and missed opportunities. We then added the collective wisdom of some very smart professionals and legendary consultants. All of this then coalesced with my personal leadership journey. It has been an amazing ride! From these many threads of inquiry and experience, we have created a tapestry of insight, inspiration, and action every leader can use to scale his or her impact.

In the subtitle of this book, we deliberately chose the word *scale* when referring to your impact. I want to help you experience exponential growth in your impact in a very short period of time. The four Smart Choices we're about to explore, if made consistently, can deliver on this audacious promise.

Smart Leadership is not dependent on your IQ, your education, or your role or level in your organization. The choices are not bound by situation or circumstance. Therefore, these choices are within reach for every leader at every level. Smart Leaders make Smart Choices.

Just as Indy surmised when looking for a life-giving cup, often the simplest is the most significant. The truth is these simple choices may well give your leadership the new life you've been searching for. Simple, however, should never be confused with easy. Focus and diligence will be required to consistently make Smart Choices and become a Smart Leader.

I honestly believe each of these Smart Choices will stand the test of time, not because they are flashy, gilded, or adorned with precious stones but because they are simple and based on timeless principles. I think that is good news for you, me, and every leader on the planet.

Here's what I will promise you: There is inherent value in each of the Smart Choices—untold power you can harness and deploy at will. There is even *greater* potential in the choices *collectively*; together they form a virtuous cycle of life-giving insight, energy, and vitality. As you learn to make these *four* choices your default response on a daily basis, your life, leadership, and legacy will be transformed forever.

SWIMMING IN QUICKSAND

"If I were to let my life be taken over by what is urgent, I might very well never get around to what is essential."
Henri Nouwen

You were just doing your job, enjoying the role, generating outstanding results, and then you received a raise (which you deserved), then another, and maybe another. One day, your boss, or your boss's boss, called you into her office. The conversation may have sounded something like this:

> We've been watching you. You're doing an outstanding job. You tackle every project with energy and optimism. Most importantly, you make things happen. Thanks for your contributions. We want you to lead this new team (or turn around a struggling one). What do you say?

Depending on the size of the task and your level of confidence, you either said *yes*, or *yes!* And boom! Just like that, you were a leader. Or were you? You had the title, but chances are good you had to grow into the role. Leadership requires a fundamentally different skill set than being an outstanding individual contributor. But being eager to learn, grow, and prove yourself, you jumped in. Before you knew it, virtually everything changed.

Along with the pay, title, and perks came a bigger job with more responsibility. Then, slowly at first, you began to realize you also had more work to do, more emails, more meetings, more people to serve, more projects to deliver, and more deadlines to meet. Somewhere along the way you started missing your kid's soccer games or your best friend's birthday party.

With more and more pressure to perform at work and conflicts at home, you may have found it hard to be present in the moment; often distracted, you were present but only in body. Your mind and spirit were being torn between several realities. You wanted to fulfill your obligations to your employer and your team. Still, you may have also had a deep yearning to honor the relationships that really mattered most to you, specifically, those with your family and friends.

Perhaps you began to ask sobering questions: *Can I do this for another five years? Do I want to?* You understood the seriousness of the questions and the implications of the answers.

Before I go on, admittedly, your story may be very different from the scenario above. Hopefully, it is not as dire as what I described. Or perhaps at this stage in your life and career, yours is not a story of tension, conflict, and anxiety. Maybe you are a born leader or were destined for leadership from childhood; it's entirely possible some of you entered an organization through a HIPO (high-potential) or leadership-development program with a promise of near-term leadership opportunities. But whether others chose you or you chose the profession, there is one thing I know to be true: leaders everywhere face monumental challenges on a daily basis.

QUICKSAND!

Do you ever feel like you are running in place? Does your work, which you actually enjoy, feel like it's sucking the life out of you? Do you yearn for more progress, more success, but perhaps it always feels just out of reach? Is your career, and perhaps your life, an unfulfilled promise? Have you ever stopped to consider what may be holding you back from accomplishing your goals, dreams, and aspirations of a better future? What is preventing you from leading at a higher level? I am assuming there may be multiple forces at play. Let's face it: most leaders I know are facing a growing list of challenges, many of them unprecedented. For our purposes, I've chosen to lump all these obstacles into one cold, dark, and lifeless metaphor: quicksand.

The quicksand metaphor works well in several ways. First, *we really don't see it coming.* People in quicksand arrive there by accident. No one plans to go there. Neither do you and I plan to have our careers derailed and our impact blunted by forces seemingly out of our control, but it can happen.

Second, *we feel helpless once we're in it.* With nothing to hold on to and circumstances appearing out of our control, a sense of helplessness can quickly emerge. Unlike one of the popular TV shows from the 1950s (which I'm not quite old enough to remember), Lassie, the trusted collie, will not go find help if you fall in the quicksand as she would have done for Timmy. Once you're deep in it, you feel very alone.

Finally, *quicksand is a formidable force.* I have read interviews with real people who were in actual quicksand. They explain the futility of the struggle. Getting out is really difficult. Quicksand has a tight grip. If you don't move deliberately and thoughtfully, you will sink even deeper. Flailing around without intent is not the answer. You'll discover the same principle will hold true when we begin discussing your escape plan—you must be intentional.

PERIL AT EVERY TURN

Rather than find a way out, most leaders just cope with quicksand— they learn to swim in it. Although learning to swim in quicksand is not the worst thing you can do, it has some significant downsides we will explore later in this chapter. For now, let's just say no swimmer ever won a gold medal swimming in quicksand, and neither has any leader excelled while squeezed by its grip.

In a natural setting, quicksand's basic components are sand and water. I wish the elements of the quicksand we face as leaders were as few and straightforward. Here's a short summary of what our adversary is made of.

Meetings

According to Michael Porter and Nitin Nohria from Harvard in their study of CEOs spanning twelve years, the average week contains thirty-seven meetings, accounting for 72 percent of their workweek.[1] You may not be leading a multibillion-dollar organization. Still, I'm guessing you attend a lot of meetings: meetings with your team, your supervisor, your department, your direct reports, cross-functional team meetings, project team meetings, meetings with vendors and strategic partners, meetings with candidates, and more. I've even spent a fair amount of time in meetings to plan other meetings.

Just to be clear, I'm not anti-meeting. I actually *love* productive, well-led meetings focused on improving performance. If done well, meetings can significantly multiply a leader's impact and results. Meetings to a leader are like the short game for a golfer: you drive for show; you putt for dough. The dough can be made in meetings better than any other venue. (More about successful meetings in the chapter Review Your Crew.) The best CEOs understand the power of meetings; nothing else could explain why they invest so much time in them. If meetings are not executed well, however, they can become the embodiment, and a tangible symbol, of the quicksand we are trying to avoid.

You can lose much more than time in poorly run meetings. The less obvious costs are incalculable, including poor decisions, shallow thinking often masquerading as creativity, missed or underserved opportunities, and a loss of influence and credibility for you as the leader.

Digital Communications (Email, Text, Social Media)

Another set of growing challenges we face as leaders is in the arena of digital communications. Had I written this book a decade ago, this section would have been mostly about email. But the world has changed. Now, the dam has broken, and if we're not careful, we could all drown in a digital deluge.

How big an issue is this really? I've been trying to answer that question for myself. Following are a few stats to help quantify the challenge. I will confess: some of these numbers are so large they feel almost abstract but hopefully will give you a sense that what you are feeling is not a product of your imagination.

- We tap, swipe, and click our phones 2,617 times per day.[2]
- The average smartphone user unlocks his or her phone 150 times per day.[2]
- We send or receive ninety-four texts per day, on average.[2]
- Globally, there are twenty-three *billion* text messages sent *per day*! This number continues to increase at a staggering rate—the number per day doubling during a recent twenty-four-month stretch.[3]

Regarding email: some might think email is to the modern world what snail mail was to previous generations. Yes and no. It may serve a similar purpose, but the volume is now approaching a debilitating level. The average office worker (which includes you and me) receives over a hundred emails a day and invests a quarter of every day responding to them. Estimates show 333 billion emails will be sent and received *every day* this year, and that number is predicted to reach 361 billion by 2024.[4] The rate of the challenge we face is accelerating.

Social media is also contributing to the whirlwind. As of July 2020, 3.6 billion people were active on social media, and that number is expected to rise to 4.4 billion by 2025.[5] Here are some other stats that show how embedded social media is in our lives:

- Adults spend an average of eleven hours, twenty-seven minutes per day connected to media.[6]
- Instagram has five hundred million active *daily* users. More than fifty billion photos have been uploaded on the platform so far. An estimated 71 percent of US businesses use Instagram.[7]
- YouTube users upload more than three hundred hours of new content per *minute*. Let me help you with the math—that's 18,000 hours of new content per hour, and 432,000 hours of new content *per day*! Almost five billion videos are watched on YouTube every single day. The average viewing session lasts more than forty minutes.[8]

What's the impact of all this digital media? I think it is summed up well by Nicolas Carr in his Pulitzer-nominated book *The Shallows*.

What the Net seems to be doing is chipping away my capacity for concentration and contemplation. Whether I'm online or not, my mind now expects to take in information the way the Net distributes it: in a swiftly moving stream of particles. Once I was a scuba diver in the sea of words. Now I zip along the surface like a guy on a Jet Ski.[9]

Constant Distractions

If, by some chance, you're reading this book at work, you've likely been interrupted during these first few pages. According to one study, the average office worker is interrupted every three minutes and five seconds. This means almost twenty times per hour, someone or something causes our brain to shift. The most troubling part of this is the time required for our brain to refocus on the task at hand—some research would indicate to fully recover our previous level of attention requires more than twenty minutes.[10] The staggering cost: our work is completed without our focused energy. Hard to imagine how much better our work could be if we could create the right environment to focus, think, and lead.

Growing Complexity

The final bucket of sand in our toxic mix, let's just call it the rise in general complexity. The world is now more complex than at any point in recorded history. Progress and complexity appear to march hand in hand. Here are a few random examples that illustrate this complexity:

- More than fifty-six billion webpages indexed through Google[11]
- More than 4.5 million apps on the iPhone and Android platforms[12]
- More than four million parts in a modern jetliner[13]
- More than 2.2 million books published annually[14]
- More than a thousand cereal brands in the United States alone[15]
- More than 185 cable TV channels in the average US home[16]

Complexity is not going to subside. It will only increase. These are just a few of the escalating challenges the modern leader must endure, evade, and ultimately escape from if we want to scale our impact in the world.

YOUR PERSONAL QUICKSAND

Before we begin to detail the escape plan I've promised, I want to address something you may be thinking:

The quicksand you just described doesn't resonate with me. My days are not dominated by meetings, distractions, and the complexity you outlined.

If none of what I've presented are challenges you're facing, then what is limiting your impact? What is impeding your success? What is thwarting your plans? What is hindering your progress? The answer to these questions is *your* quicksand.

While researching and writing this book, our team interviewed many leaders who understand the quicksand as previously described but personally were battling different issues. Here's a quick inventory of several other obstacles you may have already faced, are now facing, or will likely face in the future on your quest for more impact.

Success

Here's a fact very few are willing to embrace: success is a lousy teacher. Success does not drive progress—on the contrary, it is often its chief adversary. Only a special leader continues to push and work when you have already accomplished, or have even exceeded, your goals. However, you must overcome your current level of success to succeed at a higher level. It may feel counterintuitive, but the success you've worked so hard to achieve is likely to be one of the obstacles you must confront if you want to scale your impact.

Complacency

Often complacency is a derivative of success but not always. Sometimes complacency finds its strength in the absence of vision, the challenges of today, or the resignation that can come with a modicum of success. The best leaders I know push through this—often with the help of others. We'll discuss several strategies for overcoming complacency in the pages to follow.

Inertia

Change is hard. This is not the last time I will use this phrase in this book. Creating positive change can feel like pushing a boulder up a very steep hill. And to make matters worse, make one misstep and you can find yourself back at the bottom; if you are lucky, you can avoid being crushed by the boulder as you fall. Sometimes we find ourselves as the lone voice on a thoroughly entrenched issue or the sole agent calling for change in a behemoth of an organization. These are things that can paralyze a leader. It's just another form of quicksand.

Fatigue

Because change is hard, and for many other reasons, sometimes a leader just gets tired. I would be so bold as to say that at some point *every* leader gets tired. The question is: Can we overcome the moment or the season we find ourselves in? Can we prevent fatigue from becoming chronic? If it does, our energy for change is gone, and we've succumbed to yet another form of quicksand that is just as debilitating as all the other types.

Fear

What did William Shakespeare, George Patton, and Vince Lombardi all agree on? They all said some version of "Fear makes cowards of us all." Sometimes it's our fear that constrains us. Our fear can blind us to opportunity and rob us of the courage required to lead well. The prison that prohibits many leaders from their preferred future and the legacy they long to create is fear—fear of the unknown, fear of failure, fear of public opinion, and more.

For many leaders, fear is the agent that binds all the elements of our quicksand together to create the toxic concoction. I'm probably not the first to tell you this, but before you read another word, let me assure you: you can overcome your fear.

Aimlessness

I know this may sound strange, and I'm not trying to question your leadership, but I do have a few questions for you. Do you have a credible, actionable plan to scale your influence? Does your plan include specific tactics that work? Are you acting strategically or sporadically? I am convinced many leaders remain stuck in quicksand—busy but not thriving; trying but not changing their world, at least not at a pace they are pleased with—because they lack intentionality. If this is *your* limiting factor, your quicksand, you're in luck. The answers are available—keep reading!

Circumstances

A final form of personal quicksand many battle on a daily basis finds its genesis in circumstances totally out of their control. Our recent global pandemic, which much of the world is still struggling with, is a classic example. Millions of lives have been lost and trillions of dollars in economic value have evaporated while the pain and suffering has been incalculable. Quicksand not of our own making can be one of the most debilitating of all. However, we cannot forfeit our agency. If we do, we can lose more than our impact—we can lose our leadership. Our choices still matter.

Regardless of the quicksand you face, every leader has multiple elements warring against his or her effectiveness. Scaling your impact is not easy, but it is possible. We'll address all the forms of quicksand mentioned above and perhaps a few more throughout the pages that follow. Hang in there. There is a way out.

THE VILLAIN

Now, if you know anything about story structure, you may think I just introduced the villain in this real-life drama: the quicksand of busyness, distraction, complacency, fear, and their companions. These things are certainly the raw ingredients of the quicksand a leader must navigate, but they are not the villains. You and I are. This is not a story of man against the elements. It's a story of leaders against themselves.

I admit it can feel like us against the world (and all the forces I just reviewed). Even the quicksand analogy makes it seem like the problem is out there assaulting us. And to prove it, just like quick-sand, when you try to work your way free, it tightens its grip on you. It, the quicksand, must certainly be the problem.

Not so fast. What have you done as a leader in response to the quicksand? I have seen three primary scenarios, each with vastly different outcomes:

1. Learn to Swim (Lead) in the Quicksand

I believe the vast majority of leaders in the world are in this category. Your heart is right, your commitment is high, and your determina-tion is off the chart. You're a leader. You know it, and you're going to act like it. "When the going gets tough, the tough get going" may even be your mantra. Just keep swimming! The problem with this approach is multifaceted.

First, toughing it out and swimming in quicksand is really inefficient. You're wasting a lot of energy and probably not making nearly as much progress as you could if you were on the dry high ground. While you might survive for a season if you are a really good swimmer (leader), you will never thrive over the long term.

Next, swimming in quicksand is exhausting and unsustainable. You know as well as I do that leadership is hard. And there will likely be seasons during your career in which the demands of your role will be brutal. However, a career, and a life, in quicksand is a guar-anteed way to reduce your impact—the exact opposite of what I'm trying to help you do. To lead well will require you to be energetic, clearheaded, and focused. A perennial state of fatigue is not the pos-ture you need for sustained success.

Finally, swimming in quicksand fails to leverage your full lead-ership potential. You have so much to offer. You have a grand vision. You want to maximize your contribution and your impact. You can-not reach your full potential or give your best if you are spending your days in the soup we've just described.

2. Give Up and Die

Not literally but figuratively. When you give up and give in, your leadership and impact evaporate—maybe not instantaneously, but the slow death of your influence is inevitable. These are the women and the men who have stopped fighting, stopped struggling, and stopped swimming. In actuality, they have stopped leading. As you know, not everyone with the title fills the role. I know if you are reading this book, you are not in this group.

3. Escape the Quicksand

These are the leaders we all want to emulate. They have found a way to higher ground. Helping you plan your escape is what this book is about. I started to say rescue, but that would imply someone else is going to pull you out. That's not going to happen. No one is going to save you but you.

As I shared in the introduction, *your* choices determine your success. Now, the world may be conspiring against you, but you have so much more power and control than you think. You may feel like the victim, but you are culpable if you choose to stay in the quicksand. Rather than succumb, you can become the hero of your own story. On the following pages, the men and women who have successfully navigated these trials before us will serve as our guides.

The fact that quicksand exists is not up for debate. Neither is its assault on your life and leadership a sign of your weakness. The fact you have not yet escaped its grip is not an indicator of your fit for your role. The quicksand doesn't have to limit you or define you. It just is. What is on the table is how you will choose to respond.

You can choose to stay in the quicksand of mediocrity, exhaustion, and helplessness, or you can move to the high ground of increased influence, opportunity, and impact. Countless others made a successful escape, and they have left clues for the rest of us to follow. But first, you have to decide if you really want to be free or not. It really is your choice.

BE SMART!

Identify your quicksand. What are the top three obstacles or impediments keeping you from leading from the high ground? Write these down or put them in your phone for reference. I want you to revisit them often as you go through the content of this book. By the time you get to the end, you will have a credible plan to escape their grip.

Also, I would love to hear about your quicksand. If you want to drop me an email or text, that would be great. My email is mark@SmartLeadershipBook.com and my cell number is 678-612-8441. I hope to hear from you.

YOUR REAL
SUPERPOWER

*"Between stimulus and response there is a space. In that space is our power
to choose a response. In our response lies our growth and our freedom."*
Viktor Frankl

'll confess, as a child, I did not grow up with superheroes in my
life. I know many in my generation were influenced by Batman,
Superman, and the Hulk. I vaguely remember a few TV episodes
of Batman, but generally, I missed it. Perhaps I just wasn't paying
attention or was distracted by all my trips to the baseball field.

Now, late in my life, I am being introduced to this world for the
first time. I'm working with a former creative director from Marvel
to turn some of my previous content into graphic novels for a new
generation of leaders. The work is ongoing and has been a blast. As
we brainstormed potential superpowers for our fictional characters,
I was struck by the fact that every human being on the planet has at
least one superpower—the power to make choices.

Before I unpack this, let me quickly say that I understand not
everyone in the world has the same access to choices. I have worked
in many emerging countries where a Western (American) view of
choices is totally out of sync with their reality. I've walked the slums

of Nairobi and visited the ghettos of Mumbai; the concept of choices is very different in these situations.

I am also beginning to understand the injustices of the past which have limited the choices of many people of color in America. Restoring these choices that many of us take for granted will require bold and courageous leadership. I pray for a day justice and equality will be a reality for all people.

And finally, I know that socioeconomic factors have a huge effect on choices—families living in the grip of poverty aren't debating where to go on vacation. Those who struggle with food insecurity would scoff, rightfully so, at many of the choices we deliberate and debate, because for them, survival is the only goal.

Hopefully, problems such as these, and others, will be addressed as more leaders learn how to scale their impact. Smart Leaders are the levers required to improve our world.

Even with these exceptions and qualifiers, I'm still in the camp that the ability to make choices should be among our most prized human abilities.

Choices give us agency and opportunity. Our choices don't always generate the results we desire, but they are still *our* choices. We decide. As a leader, I love this, and I'm guessing you do too. Win or lose, we chose our path. I think that's one of the reasons leadership is so satisfying for many, not because we did it—in most cases, our team actually did it. But we played a critical role, often making the critical strategic choices to set the team up for success. We selected them, trained them, empowered them, encouraged them, coached them, resourced them, held them accountable, and more. All of these are choices we make as leaders.

But here's the dark side about our choices—not all of them are strategic, thoughtful, proactive, and productive. And sometimes we just make the wrong call. This book is not concerned with any of those situations. Every leader makes a bad call from time to time. Rather than focus on these inevitable missteps, this book is about the choices that help us make better choices. Let's explore why some choices have disproportionate impact.

SMART CHOICES

All choices are not the same. Some are high stakes, with staggering consequences, others are mundane and trivial, and a few of our choices have extended reach and influence. These few, far-reaching choices impact other choices, creating ripple effects in your life and leadership. This type of choice will be our focus and provide the story arc for this book. If applied consistently, they will also create the story arc of your influence and determine your legacy. These are what I call Smart Choices.

What this chapter, and to some extent this entire book, is really about is raising your awareness and your personal discipline regarding the choices you make. Here's why:

Choices are the most important topic you rarely think about.

If choices are so important, why don't leaders think more about them? The short answer is the brain. Research indicates that more than 90 percent of our decisions are made without conscious thought. I find this shocking and terrifying. However, the research also indicates we still make about 35,000 "remotely conscious" choices every day.[1] The best leaders work to optimize these choices.

Our process for making choices is complex to say the least. One of our researchers said the more she explored the topic, the deeper the hole became. Every decision we make is informed by many factors, conscious and subconscious. The subconscious factors, such as bias, emotions, and instincts, drive more of our decisions than our conscious choices. This fact raises the stakes for our deliberate choices; it is important to exercise our agency where we can. Here are a few findings about the mystery and magic behind our choices.

Emotions

Our *emotions* drive more of our decisions than we will ever admit. Even when we attempt to make a rational decision, it cannot be made completely isolated from our emotions. Decisions are made in the innermost parts of our brains, the limbic region. This region is not capable of language but is the seat of our decisions and emotions.

Because decisions are made in one part of the brain and language resides in another, sometimes we feel a disconnect. Simon Sinek describes this situation in one of his TEDx talks like this: "Yes, we've heard the facts, but yet, we are not convinced. When this happens, we may say, 'It just doesn't *feel* right,' or 'My gut is telling me something else.' These statements reflect the emotions which inform, and often drive, our decisions."[2]

Baba Shiv, marketing professor at Stanford and neuroeconomics expert, goes a step further. He suggests that often our rational decisions are merely the rationalizations of emotional decisions made by our limbic brains.[3]

Values and Beliefs

Our values and beliefs impact our decisions in profound ways. Again, some of these are conscious and some unconscious decisions. This is why I encourage every leader to invest the time to articulate their personal values and help their team do the same. Naming a thing can increase focus, intentionality, and diligence. Values stated become an active reference point for our choices. Vague, ambiguous, ill-defined values and beliefs are like driving in a terrible storm with extremely low visibility.

Rewards

Our brains' desire for rewards also impacts our decisions, and often, we don't understand the root of our motivation. The chemical our brain is addicted to is dopamine—a shot of mental affirmation generated as an internal reward and what many social media and technology companies are built upon. Every like, share, comment, and new follower rewards our brains. As a result, we keep clicking, posting, and checking our devices.

Cognitive Bias

Our personal cognitive biases are also a factor. Some of our biases we see and manage; my bias to move quickly and to focus on results are two that come to mind. Because I am aware of these, I can attempt to compensate. Compensation is a proven strategy, but it only works with *known* biases. The far trickier, more insidious, are the deep-seated tendencies we do not acknowledge.

There are many categories and types of cognitive biases, including omission bias, confirmation bias, self-serving bias, decline bias, and belief bias. I found one source that listed twenty-four different types of bias. The challenge is to unearth and manage as many as you can. This is where trusted voices can help you own your biases and keep them in check the best you can when making important choices.

Past Experiences

Our past experiences, good or bad, are also a factor in our choices. The brain is a self-optimizing system. What this means in its simplest form is we learn from our past and have a hardwired disposition to return to what is "known," even in the face of new information or changing circumstances. This tendency is even more pronounced if our past experience was extreme—either very positive or very negative. If it was negative, we may default to an avoidance response.

Fear

Fear deserves its own mention as a factor in the choices we make. Depending on your personality, temperament, relative risk tolerance, and past experiences, fear can be a huge factor in many of our decisions—even if we have no personal history with the choice at hand.

Individual Differences

Individual differences are important as well. Your age, geography, socioeconomic standing, faith tradition, education, and culture all impact your decisions. And as with previous contributing factors, you may or may not be aware of these influences.

Environment

Finally, your environment matters. This includes peer pressure, perceived urgency, decision overload, and decision fatigue.

On the point of decision fatigue, one study from 2010 by Levav and Danziger found that 70 percent of prisoners appearing before a parole board before lunch were granted parole and only 10 percent were given the same decision later in the day.[4] Maybe it was the time of day; maybe the panel members were just tired and hungry. Either way, the primary factor impacting the choice of the board was environmental, not fact-based.

On the pressure we can feel from others, one classic study conducted by psychologist Solomon Asch found that 75 percent of adults would give an answer they knew to be incorrect if others in the group were giving the same incorrect answer, in order to fit in.[5] Bizarre but true.

———

With so much of our choice-making process out of our conscious control and a by-product of so many factors, is it really worth the effort for leaders to focus more attention and energy on our choices? Absolutely!

Our research over the last few years has focused on a few strategic questions: What separates elite leaders from all the rest? Are these differences transferable? If so, what best practices can help you and me raise our level of leadership? Here's our conclusion, despite all the factors mentioned above: *Smart Leaders make Smart Choices.*

ALL CHOICES ARE NOT CREATED EQUAL

Have you ever given much thought to the different types of decisions we make over the course of a day or week? Smart Choices are only part of the mix.

For our purposes, and to draw your attention to the Smart Choices you and I face every day, let's review four types of choices we encounter on a regular basis, choices we do have direct, conscious influence over:

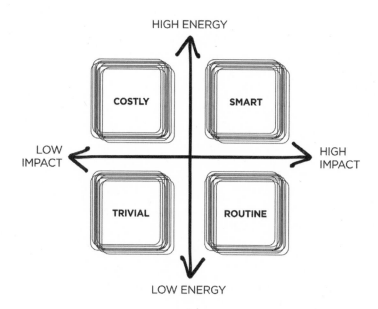

Trivial

Trivial choices are those requiring little thought, energy, or attention; these have little impact on your leadership and contribution to the world. Examples include what you will have for dinner tonight and whether you should wear blue jeans or black ones.

Costly

Costly choices are those we tend to overinvest in that have low impact. They may be important at some level but are just not of major consequence in the greater scheme of things. Examples of these include the following: What color should we paint the kitchen? Where will we go on vacation? What will I dress up as for Halloween? What enhancements can I make to the tenth draft of this PowerPoint presentation? At some point, your good intentions reach a point of diminishing returns.

Routine

Routine choices can have real consequences, yet they require very little if any focus and energy from us. Many of the 35,000 daily choices mentioned previously occur here. In this domain you will find both unique and recurring choices. If these choices are ingrained, we call them habits. Activities such as brushing your teeth, regular exercise, and saving for retirement fall into this category.

Smart

Smart Choices are the ones with high impact that require the most focus and energy to make them. Choices such as hiring a life coach, moving across the country, or starting a family all fall in this category. And as stated previously, if you can keep your eye on these choices and choose wisely, you will experience multiple benefits—you can even escape the quicksand that is slowly suffocating your influence.

THE FOUR SMART CHOICES

For now, I'll do a fifty-thousand-foot overview of the four Smart Choices. Then, on the pages to follow, you'll find a deep dive on each choice as well as two supporting chapters for each one outlining specific best practices to help you transform your good intentions into action.

Notice each choice, successfully made, leads to another choice—a virtuous cycle. The individual choices have inherent value, but the real power is released, and your impact multiplied, when you make *all four* choices.

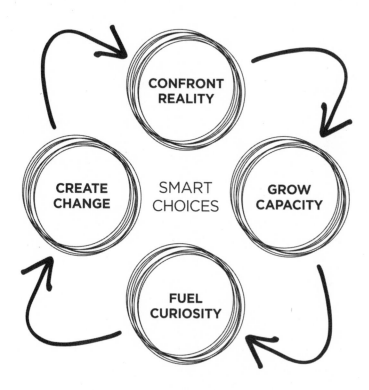

Smart Choice #1: Confront Reality

Confront Reality to stay grounded in truth
and lead from a position of strength.

Reality is a leader's most precious ally. What is true about you, your team, your organization, and your industry matters. Unfortunately, many leaders are reluctant to confront their reality. There are many potential reasons for this avoidance, and we will explore some of them on the pages that follow. However, the reasons for dodging reality never outweigh the value of confronting it. Granted, sometimes reality is hidden and must be discovered; other times it is veiled, twisted, or mangled so what remains only vaguely resembles the truth. Of the four Smart Choices we are going to explore over the balance of this book, I would suggest you think of this choice as first among equals. Imagine a scenario in which you are attempting to navigate unfamiliar terrain and your only tool is a map. Consider the difficulty in reaching your destination if you are unaware of your current position. Even an accurate and detailed map is of little value without knowledge of your starting point. Your current reality is your starting point. That is why the best leaders choose to Confront Reality.

Smart Choice #2: Grow Capacity

Grow Capacity to meet the demands of the moment and the challenges of the future.

I remember a conversation I had with a young leader years ago. He was very talented and full of potential. He came to me one day with a question: "Do you and other senior leaders talk a lot about people who have hit their capacity limits?" I told him we rarely discussed those people. He seemed a bit confused. I then added, "We talk a lot about men and women who have found ways to expand their capacity." The best leaders are constantly looking for ways to increase their influence and impact. They realize, either instinctively or through coaching, the path to maximum contribution, satisfaction, and, ultimately, reward is paved with personal and organizational capacity. Your capacity for contribution is not finite unless you choose to limit yourself. Without capacity, the other choices can be nothing more than unfulfilled aspirations. How much time, energy, and focus can you deploy? The best leaders choose to Grow Capacity.

Smart Choice #3: Fuel Curiosity

> Fuel Curiosity to maintain relevance and vitality in a changing world.

Curiosity is a gift each of us was given at birth. Curiosity powered our early childhoods. It was the unseen force behind our questions, both stated and unstated—our desire to learn was insatiable. And then, slowly, almost imperceptibly, something began to change. With every passing year, most people become less and less curious. For many, the flame of curiosity has been virtually extinguished. However, this is not the case for the best leaders. These women and men realize leadership and learning are lifelong traveling companions. They also know, if they are able to constantly learn and grow throughout their careers, this single endeavor will become their leadership fountain of youth. There are many impediments to what may appear to be an easy choice. Success, or your current performance plateau, is a common culprit. Our past success often prevents us from an even brighter future. We must learn to learn beyond our success. The Smart Choice is to continuously Fuel Curiosity.

Smart Choice #4: Create Change

> Create Change today to ensure a better tomorrow.

To Confront Reality may be a leader's first Smart Choice, but it is not their destination. The ability to Create Change is the essence of leadership. Leadership is fundamentally about challenging what is, with an eye on what can be. You may be wondering why something so elementary and essential would need to be one of the Smart Choices. Far too many leaders accept their current reality as their destiny. Perhaps it is the quicksand, the flailing, the exhaustion—the cause of resignation varies from leader to leader. Too many leaders have lost confidence in their abilities to create a preferred future. Or, equally as tragic, they have lost sight of the vision itself. Without a compelling picture of the future, the struggle will always be too great. Therefore, to Create Change must be one of the choices—without it, there can be no true leadership.

In the pages that follow, we will do a deep dive into four specific Smart Choices. These are not the only Smart Choices you will be confronted with as a leader, but they are foundational if you want to scale your impact.

A VIRTUOUS CYCLE

Here's how the Smart Choices work together to form a lifeline for you and your leadership:

If you want to create a preferred future, you must begin with clarity regarding where you are starting the journey—the Smart Choice to Confront Reality is foundational. Putting this choice into action will help you understand your strengths and those of your team, while also identifying opportunities for improvement. This knowledge will become increasingly important as you move into an uncharted future.

To Confront Reality is a worthy beginning but of little value if you lack the needed capacity to respond appropriately. The second Smart Choice, Grow Capacity, is essential, both personally and organizationally. Increasing your personal capacity will enable you to close the gap between today and tomorrow and seize opportunities along the way.

Why would you make the first two Smart Choices if you are unable to learn, grow, and create the solutions your team and organization need? If you do not stay relevant as a leader, you will be ill-prepared and ultimately left behind. Yesterday's solutions have a decreasing half-life in an ever-changing world. Only when you choose to Fuel Curiosity can you maintain the vitality and creativity required to be an effective leader of tomorrow.

And finally, what good are the first three choices unless you actually step into a preferred future? To do this always requires a leader willing to Create Change. Many would-be world beaters are defeated at the doorstep of greatness because they do not choose to move passionately and courageously toward their vision.

You and I have far more influence over our futures and our levels of impact than we think we do. If you have doubts, that's understandable; stay with me for a few more chapters. If, at that point, you disagree with my premise, you can go back to your version of normalcy.

I hope for your sake, and those you lead, you will not retreat. The status quo is always a hollow and fragile substitute for a vibrant future. For me, I would rather invest my life and leadership striving to create a better world.

For all of us, this journey begins, and is sustained, with a few strategic, life-and-leadership-altering choices. Like the first dominos in a chain reaction of ever-increasing impact—tip them over and watch what happens.

YOUR CHOICES MATTER!

As you begin this book and make your final determination as to whether you are going to *finish* this book, I want us to be on the same page on one critical issue: Why would anyone want to do the things outlined in this book? More specifically, why would *you* want to take this journey?

You are a leader who wants to make a difference in the world. You have a dream, or a vision, or a calling to change your world—many of you can already see it, you can almost touch it, but as of yet, it doesn't exist. Well, that's not totally true. It does exist in your head, heart, and imagination. You can see it as clearly as anything you have ever seen with your physical eyes. It is very real even though it is not yet reality. The problem you face is multifaceted. As we just reviewed, there are forces at play conspiring to steal your dreams and render you helpless. The four Smart Choices that serve as the cornerstones of this book are your way forward.

No leader makes any of the choices we are about to explore for the fun of it. (Although you may find some of the choices more fun than others.) We do it because these choices will help us scale our impact, accelerate our journey, expand our influence, increase our ability to serve others, and realize our dreams. The Smart Choices are the ticket to accomplish *your* goals. That's why you should read this book cover to cover.

BE SMART!

You are no stranger to the Smart Choices outlined in this chapter. What is required for you to scale your impact is to *more consistently* make these choices. Identify at least one time in your life or leadership in which you made each one of the four Smart Choices. You have done it before. You can do it again and again.

CONFRONT
REALITY

CONFRONT REALITY

"The first responsibility of a leader is to define reality."
Max Dupree

As legend has it, one day long ago, a young man came to Socrates and said, "I need you to help me find knowledge."

Socrates said, "Let's take a walk." As they walked along the beach, Socrates said nothing. Then the would-be apprentice was a bit startled as Socrates began to walk out into the water. Unsure what to do next, he hastily followed him. Once they were submerged chest high in the gentle waves, Socrates stopped and turned to face his new student. "Tell me again what you want from me."

"I want you to help me find knowledge," said the slightly confused young mentee. As the story is told, Socrates then grabbed the man by his shoulders and pushed him around under the water and held him there for longer than one might expect.

Upon resurfacing, the man, obviously startled, coughing and spitting out the warm Mediterranean water, said, "What are you doing?"

Socrates calmly responded, "Now tell me again: What do you want from me?"

"As I said before, I want you to help me find knowledge."

As soon as the last word came from the man's lips, Socrates grabbed him again and pushed him under the water, this time keeping him submerged even longer!

As the story goes, this happened several more times. On each subsequent plunge, Socrates held the man underwater even longer. And the last time he did it, the man came out of the water and in response to Socrates's now often repeated question, "What do you want from me?" the man gasped, "I want air!"

Socrates responded, "When you want knowledge as badly as you want air, you will find it."

For our purposes I want to paraphrase the wisdom of Socrates. When you want to know reality as much as you want air, you will find it. Our first Smart Choice is to Confront Reality.

Max Dupree, the former CEO of the legendary furniture company Herman Miller, said, "The first responsibility of a leader is to define reality."

For some of you, this may sound too obvious. You are probably eager to say, "Check! I do that. What else do you have for me?" This may be your situation, but I meet leaders all the time who are not confronting reality.

Have you ever known a leader who was not willing to confront the truth? Maybe he or she didn't want to own up to their own leadership shortcomings. Perhaps they did not want to address poor performing team members or a failed strategy. Some leaders are unwilling to address issues outside the workplace, including poor health, toxic relationships, and unwise financial decisions, to name a few.

If you and I were sitting down over a cup of coffee, I would ask you to tell me *their* story. Together, we would play the role of coach, consultant, and pop psychologist and have some fun creating our own hypothesis as to why the leader in question behaved as they did. Who knows? We might be able to figure out why the leader under analysis was unwilling to confront reality.

AVOIDING THE TRUTH

I'm sorry we can't have that conversation, but I have posed the question to many leaders: "Why do so many leaders have trouble confronting reality?" Here are some of their responses.

Fear of Failure

Who wants to fail? Not me. Not you. But mature leaders see failure differently than most people. When I am honest with myself, I know I *need* a modicum of failure in my life—and you do too. If I'm not failing from time to time, I'm not stretching enough.

Living in Denial

I'm not sure this is a root cause or not, but it is real—I've seen it. I am not a psychologist, but a leader living in denial may have other issues in play that I'm not qualified to comment on. Let's just say a leader who consistently denies the truth of his or her current reality, for whatever reason, is not leading from a position of strength.

Arrogance

Some leaders' confidence is so great, they cross the line and become arrogant. She or he knows so much (in their own minds) that they can, in essence, create their own twisted version of reality. This is never a formula for success. It suboptimizes results, erodes confidence, and destroys trust.

Life Is Good

The more successful a leader is, the more challenging it can become to confront unpleasant or unflattering realities. When your team is working well, your organization is gaining market share, and your income is at an all-time high and rising, a clear picture of reality can become a nuisance. Successful people can sometimes be the worst students.

Short-Term Thinking

As Marshall Goldsmith so famously said, "What got you here won't get you there." However, if a leader's time horizon is too short, he or she will have extreme difficulty embracing truth that runs counter to their *current* reality. These are leaders who will always be surprised when their organizations are lagging behind competitors who invested in the future when they did not.

Appearance Over Performance

If you are truly concerned about performance, understanding and confronting your reality is perhaps your best friend. What's working? What's not? How well am I leading? What could I do differently? However, if you are merely attempting to imitate a leader, trying to maintain appearances, the truth of your reality becomes an inconvenience to be avoided.

Too Busy

If we are not careful, we can allow our pace to blind us to the reality of our lives and our leadership. Unfortunately, I see this all the time—activity and accomplishment are not synonymous. You and I can easily choose the fast lane to self-destruction. One of the first casualties on this path is the desire and ability to confront reality.

Disconnected, Disengaged, or Distracted

Tragically, some leaders are checked out—uninvolved and uninterested. This may be an outcome created by their stage of life or career, affluence, or outside interests and concerns. Any of these can steal a leader's attention. Absentee leadership is not a thing. However, even physical presence is no substitute for full engagement.

Optimism

You may be surprised by this one. You would probably say optimism is one of a leader's most treasured assets. I agree. However, if we are not grounded in truth and committed to the never-ending pursuit of it, our optimism can actually be our Achilles' heel. Our belief in our team and our own leadership can make it very difficult to accept, much less confront, our reality. From time to time, "We will figure this out," or "I'm sure this will work," and other such optimistic proclamations are not only *not* based in reality but also wrong.

———

Wow! What a list! Why did I invest so much of the word count on this section? Not to discourage, but to warn you. As leaders, I think we're particularly susceptible to all of these issues. That's why smart leaders make the Smart Choice to Confront Reality.

Now, let's just suppose you and I, through a lot of self-leadership, can avoid the pitfalls I just listed. How can we activate our choice to Confront Reality?

THE SMART CHOICE

Confront Reality to stay grounded in truth
and lead from a position of strength.

Once you and I have decided to Confront Reality, there are some very tangible things we can do to make good on our choice. Here are a few of them.

Define the Universe

First, make a list of all the areas in your life where it would be really good for you to have a crystal clear picture of your current reality. I'm going to give you some examples, but *your* list will be much more helpful than what I'm about to offer.

To help get you started, here a few areas in which I believe you may want to know the truth. Because I don't know your individual situation and because we will cover some of these ideas in the upcoming chapters, I'll stay at a little higher elevation here.

- **Your Leadership.** I think it's really good for us as leaders to know the truth about our leadership. How well are we leading—really? What are our blind spots? Unless you go look for them, you won't know the answer because that's why they're called blind spots, right? I think one of our aspirations as a leader should be to make our blind spots as small as possible.

- **Your Team.** I think it would also be helpful if you knew the unvarnished truth about your team. Are they just good enough? Are they exceptional? Does your day crew rock and maybe your night crew is a little bit scary? How about your leadership team? What is true about your leadership team—collectively and the individual members?

- **Your Organization.** What's the current reality regarding your business or organization? How are you performing against your potential, not just against your peers? Are your strategies and plans generating the results you want? If you have a plan to decrease cost or to increase sales or to improve quality or to improve your safety score, how well are your strategies actually working?

- **Your Life.** What is true about your life? Are you swimming in quicksand? Are you living your life in a sustainable fashion? Can you continue to do what you are doing the way you are doing it for a decade? Two? Three? Are you participating at the level you desire at work, at home, in the community?

- **Your Relationships.** How healthy are your relationships? Are they vibrant and life-giving? Who are the people who breathe life into you? Who are the individuals who drain your energy? How can you better steward the relationships you cherish?

- **Your Finances.** How are you doing financially? Are you living within your means? Do you have debt weighing you down? How well have you prepared for your financial future? Do you have a financial plan? If so, when's the last time it was updated? Would those who know you the best say you are stewarding your financial resources well?

- **Your Health.** How's your health? Are your personal habits (e.g., diet, exercise, sleep) contributing or detracting from the life you want to lead? When's the last time you had a physical? How would your doctor describe your current state of fitness? Are you living a lifestyle that allows you to maximize your contribution to the world?

- **Your Community.** More than likely, you are having an impact beyond your work and family. If not, have you drawn your circle of influence too small? What is true about the impact you're having on your community? Are you serving intentionally? How would those in the community describe your contributions?

- **Your Spirituality.** I know this is perhaps the most personal item on this list. If you don't want to assess this area, or if you don't believe there is a spiritual realm, don't include it in your universe. However, many believe a core part of our humanity is how we relate to larger, unseen forces. Some leaders find strength and power beyond themselves and would identify this as an integral part of their success. Do you feel centered, grounded, and connected to a higher power?

- **Your Legacy.** What is the current state of your legacy? Many think about the question of legacy as if it will not be answered until decades from now—I think about it differently. Today is the latest installment in your legacy and mine. If today were your last day, how would you be remembered? Is it how you want to be remembered? Every day is a legacy-building day.

Narrow Your Focus

Your list of the areas in which you want to be grounded in reality is probably long and broad—that's wonderful. But for it to be manageable and helpful, you will need to be specific. Which of these areas do you have the most concern about? Which has the highest probability of presenting a near-term problem? Are there any of these areas in which you have already had a glimpse of your current reality but have been unwilling to confront it? Can you identify any blind spots that could derail you? These questions, and others like them, are like the Geiger counters used to find buried treasure. As you sort through these questions, I'm confident you will gain clarity regarding where to start digging.

Even though I'm sure many areas of your life and leadership are fantastic, we shouldn't paint with too big a brush. Just because one facet is fabulous doesn't mean there isn't a storm brewing somewhere else. Really good leaders live with a productive paranoia. They are constantly trying to anticipate the next threat around the corner or over the horizon.

When you are specific, when you pinpoint the object of your query, your eyesight improves drastically. Maybe you will find a real gap or perhaps an overlooked opportunity. Maybe you can leverage a personal or organizational strength you have missed in the past because you've not been focused, specific, and intentional. Once you know where you want to begin, here are a few ideas to make your search more productive.

Check the Data

This may seem like an odd and even obvious recommendation. However, it is an often-overlooked, important best practice.

Here's the deal: some of you are data people, and some of you are not. I get it. Data rarely tells the whole story, but it does tell *a* story. And it can be a vital piece of understanding a bigger picture.

I was working with a leader a few years back who was seeking my input on a new project he wanted to undertake beyond his core responsibilities. I said, "That's a wonderful vision. How's your current performance?"

He said, "Pretty good."

My follow-up question was the turning point in the conversation. "What does the data say about your performance?"

He confessed that out of thirty people on his team, his performance ranked last. "Now may not be the best time to take on something extra," I offered. Together, we discovered the answer he was seeking by looking at the data.

To be clear, I am not suggesting you can always find the answers you want in the data, but it can provide a critical piece of the puzzle. Had this gentleman's performance been more typical, we would have needed a longer conversation.

Ask Challenging Questions

I think one of the most valuable life skills a leader can acquire is the ability to ask good, thought-provoking, and challenging questions. I am such a fan of this idea you'll see an entire chapter devoted to the topic later in this book. However, I really couldn't address the idea of how to Confront Reality without a word on questions.

When I was much younger, I had an encounter with a leader I truly respected. He was an unofficial mentor as well as the president of our company. One day, I was standing in the hallway at our corporate office when he approached. Without warning, or even a "How are you?" he said, "How do you add value around here?"

Needless to say, I was a little taken aback. At that point in my career, I had been on staff for more than a decade and had led several successful teams. To tell the truth, I wasn't sure what to say.

The seconds that passed between his question and my response felt like an eternity. Unscripted and certainly not premeditated, I said, "I ask challenging questions."

He looked me square in the eye and said, "Keep it up." He turned and walked away. That was the day I decided questions would be my constant companion.

If you really want to cut through the noise, clutter, and distractions of life and gain greater clarity regarding what is really happening, good! Asking challenging questions is one of your best tools.

See for Yourself

The Japanese have a phrase for this, *Genchi Gembutsu*, literally translated as "Go see for yourself." It is one of the quality practices pioneered by Toyota. The company says they began working on their process in 1948. Go and see is not a new idea, but it is one that has stood the test of time. Data is good, reports are helpful, but there are few substitutes for leaders going to see for themselves.

Earlier in my career, I had the opportunity to spend time with Bill George at the Harvard Business School. For those who are not familiar with Bill, he is the former CEO of Medtronic, a medical device company specializing, at the time, in surgical implants. He was their CEO for twelve years. Under his leadership, their sales rose from $1 billion to $60 billion with 35 percent growth, year after year, for twelve years.[1]

His name came immediately to mind when I thought about this idea of See for Yourself. Bill shared the fact that, during his tenure as CEO, he personally observed over a thousand operations in the operating room, watching surgeons use his company's devices and implants. He said when you see a piece of your equipment malfunction and witness firsthand the life and death consequences, no one ever has to talk to you again about the importance of quality.

FIND FRESH EYES

You do not have to take this journey alone. The best leaders we talked to were always looking for allies and trusted voices to speak truth and help them stay grounded in reality.

If you gave a man who has lived in a small rural village in a developing country his entire life a million dollars to design and build a house, what are the chances the style of his new home would be French Colonial, Greek Revival, or Cape Cod? Close to zero. We create based on what we know—or think we know. Our personal experience is a formative factor in our leadership. It shapes our beliefs and our behaviors.

This phenomenon of being, in essence, trapped by our own experiences can be lethal in organizations. That's why I have always valued fresh eyes. What are fresh eyes? They are the people who possess one or more of the following attributes.

- They have a different worldview.
- They have no direct stake in the outcome.
- They work in a different discipline.
- They are from outside your organization.
- They did not create the existing system or process in question.
- They are new to the topic or subject matter being discussed.
- They are known and trusted truth tellers.
- They are not intimidated by you, your role, or your organization.

Here are some of the things you should expect from them.

- **They challenge assumptions.** This is one of the things good consultants always do. They can see things you don't. They can help you see your assumptions and the consequences of those beliefs.

- **They confront your biases.** I touched on the power of our biases in our world in the chapter Your Real Superpower. The most confounding part of bias is the fact that many, if not most, are unconscious; we are literally unaware of them. Fresh eyes can often spot a bias and make us aware of its impact in our leadership.

- **They ask the right questions.** You might assume the best questions need not come from an outsider—you would be correct. Nonetheless, it is telling how often the most challenging, paradigm-busting questions do come from an outsider.

- **They introduce new ideas.** This is one of the primary advantages someone from the outside has over the insider—they are often paid to see what's going on at other organizations. I know consultants who have worked with scores of organizations during their careers. On virtually every engagement, they discover transferable practices you and your team can apply or adapt to your situation.

- **They can get your attention.** I'll never forget one meeting with someone outside our organization—he was yelling, cursing, and knocking things off the table. That's exactly what we needed. When he amped up his energy and challenge, we ramped up our thinking.

- **They are paid to tell you the truth.** In my experience, the best consultants and executive coaches always tell the truth. The second-rate ones will tell you what you want to hear. If you're going to pay for fresh eyes—hire a truth teller. There is no value in someone with fresh eyes who won't tell you what he or she sees.

For any leader who has made the Smart Choice to Confront Reality, finding fresh eyes will make it much easier to operationalize your choice. The following are sources you may want to consider.

Personal Board of Directors

Wouldn't it be beneficial to have a group of people who could give you counsel when you had an important decision to make? To have a group of seasoned leaders who could help you evaluate opportunities and establish strategic priorities would be a real asset. And what if this group was also willing to give you feedback on your performance? You can build a group like this. Here are a few tips to maximize this strategy.

- **Make it diverse.** This is first on this list for a reason. You want and need diverse opinions. Recruit people from different disciplines, different stages in their careers, different worldviews, and so on. These should not just be a group of friends who will support every idea you want to chase.

- **Keep it small.** I don't know the *best* number, but my sense is that it is closer to five than ten. However, if you are thinking virtual and these people will never physically meet, you could enlist more. At some point, it will become unwieldy, especially when you are seeking the wisdom of the group on a specific topic.

- **Keep it fresh.** Your board will probably need to change as you move through various stages of your life and career. If you are early in life, the input of people who have more experience is crucial. At midcareer, you may want to include more people who have already transitioned to the next phase of their lives.

- **Stay in touch.** Whether virtual or physical, it will be important for you to maintain a relationship with your individual board members. This can take many forms, but you will need to be intentional. This is why many CEOs strategically invest a portion of their time on board relations.

- **Ask for feedback.** One of the best things your board can do is serve as a trusted source of feedback. Don't wait for them to offer it—ask for it. If you are not intentional and proactive, you could miss one of the biggest advantages of this structure. If you have selected the right members, they will help you Confront Reality.

- **Seek their counsel.** Feedback is about the past, and counsel is about the future. As you talk to your board about your goals, strategies, and plans, ask for their advice. Ask them to share from their experiences. Ask what about your plan concerns them. Ask them to help you succeed.

- **Help them win.** Try to add value to your board members. Introduce them to people they might like to know; share resources with them you think might be helpful; ask them a simple question: "How can I serve you?" Use your imagination and make the relationship mutually beneficial as much as possible.

Mentors

Have you had a mentor in your life? According to one study in 2018, over 40 percent of professionals have not.[2] I think this is a real missed opportunity. I dream of a world in which every leader has a mentor or a coach or both. I'll say more about coaches in the next section. But first, let's try to crack the code on why so many don't have a mentor. I think at the highest level, there are two primary reasons.

The first and most obvious reason is that many are not looking for one. If you are reading this book and don't have one or more mentors speaking truth into your life, I want to encourage you to start looking for one. However, the second reason many leaders don't have mentors in their life is the difficulty of enlisting one. Let's explore a few ideas to make the process easier.

- **Narrow your focus.** If you want a single mentor to help you with relationships, finances, career management, spiritual growth, and personal fitness, good luck! The odds of finding one person who can meet all your development needs are slim. If this is your expectation, I can understand why you may have been unsuccessful finding a mentor. What if you picked a topic and then looked for someone to help you? You may even decide you want or need multiple mentors in your life at one time.

- **Don't set the bar too high.** Let us assume you have narrowed your focus but still can't find anyone. Perhaps you have set the bar too high. The person you are looking for does not have to be the best in the world in the area you're trying to develop. In reality, they just need to be ahead of you on the journey. Rather than pursue a nationally recognized author or thought leader, try a local college professor or businessperson. Ask yourself two simple questions: Do they know more than me on the topic at hand? Are they willing to help me grow?

- **Don't ask for too much.** There are some who consider becoming a mentor a lifelong commitment. Although this is possible and I have had one mentor who invested in me for many years, this is not where I would start. If you approach someone and say, "Hi, would you be my mentor for the rest of your life?" your chances of success are limited. However, do what I've done many times and say something like this: "Can I buy you lunch?" You will likely get a very different response. You may be wondering, "Is that really a mentoring relationship?" It depends on what you discuss at lunch.

Coaches

There are many similarities between coaches and mentors. One fundamental difference: mentors work for free, and coaches work for cash. If you have never searched for a coach before, be prepared—the price range is enormous. I have a friend who would love to be your coach—for $1,000,000 per year. The good news is that we can all find a coach for far less; some start below $100 per hour.

I've had a professional coach on and off for the last few decades. And just like mentors have different areas of expertise, so do coaches. That's why I've benefited from coaching in several areas of my life over the years. I have worked with a physical conditioning and strength coach, a public speaking coach, a financial planner (coach), and a life coach. Most recently, I've hired my first golf coach. We'll see how that works out.

If you are in need of help in a specific area and have the resources, a coach may be the right path for you. These women and men are paid to tell you the truth and always bring fresh eyes to issues you may no longer be able to see clearly.

I remember the day one of my speaking coaches looked at a videotape of a talk I had given in front of a large audience—thousands of people. I knew in my heart it was not my best work, but I was full of rationalizations. I knew I was capable of better, but there were ample *excuses* I could offer to justify why I just didn't have my A game.

She wasn't buying any of it. She told me to rediscover my passion for the topic or never give that particular talk again. She was disgusted with my energy, effort, and preparation. This was a wake-up call. She reminded me that I, and I alone, am responsible for what I say and how I say it—no one else. It was painful, and it was extremely helpful. This is one reason I love a paid coach. In my experience, they are generally more concerned with the truth than the relationship (although I believe the truth is a great path to a meaningful relationship). My mentors have all been much kinder than my coaches. My life coach says, "If coaching is done well, it always gets ugly."

You will have to decide what style of coaching will be most helpful for you. What I've learned about myself is that hard truth is the best truth. It motivates me, inspires me, and changes my behavior much more efficiently than someone who sugarcoats reality. Remember: when you make the Smart Choice to Confront Reality, you want the good, the bad, and the ugly.

Consultants

I have a bias: I love working with consultants. I assume this has been informed by my good fortune to work with some outstanding ones over the years. They are usually wicked smart, ask the most thought-provoking questions, bring insights born of their vast experience, tell the truth, and help me grow. They can do the same for you.

Here are a few tips when hiring a consultant or agency.

- **Narrow your focus.** I know I've mentioned this previously, but as John Dewey said many years ago, a problem well-defined is a problem half solved. Once you know what the issue is, you'll be able to find the right consultancy to help. I prefer specialist to generalist. In my experience, a generalist may not be able to bring the rigor and deep expertise the conversation demands.

- **Hire the best you can find and afford.** If you thought the price range was broad for coaches, wait until you begin to explore the costs for consultants. The cost to engage a consultant, or a team of consultants, can easily run into the millions. Don't let this scare you. A precise problem statement, a tight project plan, and an accelerated timeline can yield fantastic results without breaking the bank.

- **Partner with them; don't delegate.** Some use consultants as an outsourcing strategy. I assume there are times when this makes perfect sense. I would rather form a partnership with outside consultants. That way, it's not just the consultants who are getting smarter; you and your team are too.

- **Learn from the experience.** Every time we finish another major project with an outside consultant, I feel like I've been back to school. If you have a chance to engage with outside experts and you don't personally grow from the experience, you missed a real opportunity.

Peer Groups

I really didn't know what to call this. Some might call it a small group, others a *mastermind group*, a term coined by Napoleon Hill over eighty years ago.[3] You might even consider it a leadership book club. Whatever you call it, if it is structured properly, your group can help you activate on the Smart Choice to Confront Reality. The idea is simple: meet regularly with a group of peers focused on a common purpose or learning objective.

Twenty-four years ago, I joined with nine other men to begin studying the topic of leadership. With very few exceptions, we have met twice a month ever since, going deep on one central question: *How do we improve our leadership so we can have a greater impact in the world?*

We celebrate, laugh, and cry together; we study, learn, fall, get back up, and serve each other. If you don't have these types of relationships in your life, I suggest you consider starting a group—whatever you call it.

NEVER STOP PURSUING

As our team contemplated the best way to convey this first Smart Choice, we debated the language for months, ultimately landing on Confront Reality. We liked the energy and the attitude it conveys. We knew the best leaders are never indifferent about the truth of their world, nor do they shy away from it. However, there is one part of this label that still concerns me.

To *confront* could be misconstrued as a *singular* event—do it and check it off. We can *never* stop seeking what is true about our world. Our reality is constantly in flux, dynamic, never static. Therefore, we must always pursue the current reality with a dogged determination. When we find what is true about our leadership, our team, and our world, we must be willing to *confront* it—again and again and again.

Obviously, there are many strategies and virtually unlimited tactics you can use in your quest to stay grounded in reality. What's most important is your commitment to finding the truth—no matter where it leads you. Although our reality is all around us, it isn't always obvious—it often lurks in disguise, evading our casual glances. And it always shuns our half-hearted efforts to expose it. The best leaders know this, and now, so do you.

———

A few years ago, I had my first physical. The experience was organized such that I would go from station to station and room to room for the various tests. I started with the treadmill; that didn't go well. I was humbled when the technician began to increase the incline. My day was not off to a good start.

By the end of the day, I had failed virtually every aspect of my physical. I failed the treadmill test, I failed the breathing test, and I couldn't get my body to sink in the tank where they measure body fat. I even failed the hearing test. Upon learning this, I asked the technician for a note. When he asked why, I said, "When my wife suggests I am not listening to her, I can give her the note to remind her of my condition." I mean, I failed, I failed, and I failed.

Well, here's the truth of that day. For me, the physical exam had no real value—it had no power to improve my health. It was an event, a mere moment in time, nothing more than a snapshot of my condition at that point. The *real* value of any assessment, and the truth you can discover, is what you do with it. Your current reality is not your destination—it is only the starting point.

Since that moment in time, I have run a marathon, climbed mountains, and done a number of things that would certainly have seemed impossible based on the reality of that day. Never be fearful of your current reality—embrace it, learn from it, and get ready to take action. What is true today does not have to define your tomorrow. It is only where you must begin.

BE SMART!

Make your own list of areas in which you need to Confront Reality. Write out what you believe to be true in each of those areas today. Next, write what you want to be true in each of those areas. Begin making your plans to attack the gaps.

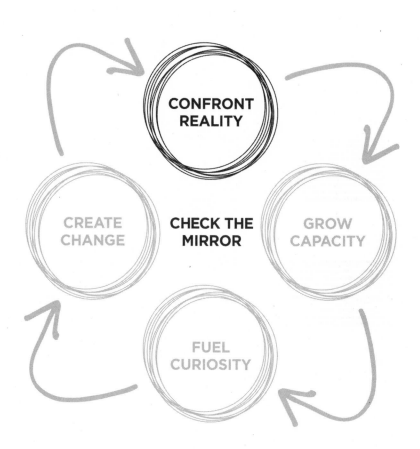

CONFRONT
REALITY

CREATE
CHANGE

CHECK THE
MIRROR

GROW
CAPACITY

FUEL
CURIOSITY

CHECK THE MIRROR

"The unexamined life is not worth living."
Socrates

Kristen Hadeed founded Student Maid in 2009 while a college student at the University of Florida. On day three of her new start-up, forty-five of her sixty employees quit. As she tells the story, it was not the work, the heat, or the hours; she was the reason they were quitting. She was "giving hugs rather than feedback, fixing errors instead of enforcing accountability, and hosting parties instead of cultivating meaningful relationships." Her approach to leadership was literally killing her company—fast!

Kristen has learned much since that first week. Today, her company has sales of more than $30 million annually. What changed? Kristen says she learned quickly that leadership is not permission to do less but signing up to do more. She had to change the way she thought about her role and then show up differently.[1]

Have you ever had such clarity about your leadership? I hope so. If not, perhaps this chapter will help. After you have made the Smart Choice to Confront Reality, you have to turn that aspiration into action. Hopefully, you made a list of areas in which the truth would be helpful to enhance your impact. This chapter is intended to provide some very practical strategies and tactics for evaluating and improving your leadership.

Peter Drucker said to "know thyself" is one of the prerequisites to lead well;[2] yet many leaders don't really know themselves at all. Research indicates the higher you move in an organization, the less self-aware you are.[3] This is why you need to check the mirror.

Checking the mirror is about you—not your team, your organization, your shareholders, your competition, or anyone else. This is about a long, hard look at your performance and the way you lead, then confronting the reality staring back at you. Let's start with your picture of leadership—do you have one? It may prove helpful as you decide what to assess and what to evaluate.

My picture of leadership is an iceberg. You probably remember from grade school your teacher's description of the iceberg, with only 10 percent of it showing above the waterline and 90 percent remaining below. If you were like me, you thought, *No way! How is that possible?* I went to Antarctica to see for myself. Even after seeing it, I don't understand the science behind the phenomenon, but it still creates a perfect picture of leadership. About 10 percent of your leadership—your skills—is above the waterline, and about 90 percent—your leadership character—remains out of sight.

This paradigm informs my questions when I look in the mirror; I need to look at my skills *and* my leadership character.

ASK THE RIGHT QUESTIONS

What follows are questions to ask yourself in order to begin improving these critical facets of your leadership. Let's stare into the mirror for a while.

How Well Do You See the Future?

Leadership always begins with a picture of the future. Vision, as we'll cover in depth in the chapter See the Unseen, is about seeing what others don't and believing it. Leaders are the architects of the future, but we must see the future before we can rally others to build it. This is the part of leadership where your intuition, experience, judgment, creativity, knowledge of your business and industry, and your courage collide to paint an irresistible picture of a preferred future. Don't make the common mistake of assuming this is someone else's job. The difference between the CEO's vision and the frontline leader's is breadth and time horizon, but both still need vision to lead well. Leaders must invest enough time in the future to ensure their organization has one.

How Engaged Are the People You Lead?

Many organizations are starving while sitting on a sandwich. There is so much untapped potential in the people you have already hired. However, engagement remains a riddle most leaders have yet to solve. You may well be aware of the annual research conducted by Gallup on the state of the American workforce (they actually do this study globally). Each year for the last twenty years, the engagement level of our workers has been abysmal. The 2020 survey showed 64 percent of employees in the United States are not engaged at work.[4] Imagine the loss of competitive advantage and human potential. These results are not the product of an apathetic workforce. Rather, they are the result of leaders who are not willing to confront and correct this issue.

What Is Your Track Record on Reinvention?

One of my fun memories is from an afternoon I spent with John Wooden, the legendary coach of the UCLA men's basketball program. On the day we visited with the coach at his condo in Westwood, he was still fully engaged—and engaging, no small feat when you are over ninety years old.

One of the stories from the coach that I believe provides a clue to his enduring greatness and unrivaled record was his annual improvement project. His practice each off-season was to study one facet of the game. He would watch film, read books, and interview coaches and top performers—one year, he studied dribbling; another season, he focused on rebounding. He was always willing to reinvent his methods and his thinking for the sake of improvement. Coach embraced the truth: progress is always preceded by change.

How Well Do You Value Results and Relationships?

I've been taking an unscientific poll with leaders around the world on this topic for twenty years. Here's my conclusion: valuing both results and relationships may be the most difficult aspect of leadership for you—it is for the vast majority of leaders. Having thought about this for a long time, I'll share my opinion as to why—you can agree or not.

I believe most leaders have a natural bias. They are either more results-oriented or more relationship-oriented. This is not a good or bad thing, but the trick is to value both. If you don't, you will suboptimize your contribution and the performance of whatever and whoever you are attempting to lead. The path to valuing both is one of compensation. Think of it like a prescription for eyeglasses or contacts. Eyeglasses are intended to help you compensate for something you don't naturally do well (see up close or far away). My challenge and yours is to employ the right compensatory practices so we can value *both* results *and* relationships.

How Well Do You Live Your Values?

Core values are a powerful tool in a leader's toolbox. They are like a Swiss Army knife. You can use them to shape a culture in many ways. They can be used to assess would-be employees, onboard those who make it through the selection process, train employees on desired behaviors, evaluate these same employees, form the basis for recognition programs, and more. However, there's a catch. If the leaders don't model these same values, trust in the leader will erode, and the desired behaviors will be diminished, not elevated. If this behavior persists, the leaders in question will ultimately forfeit the opportunity to lead. People always watch the leader.

Are You a Lifelong Learner?

What enables some leaders to lead at an extremely high level for decades? The Smart Choices are obviously at play. However, this question is intended to call out one defining characteristic of the best leaders—they are learners. However, there is no formula—leaders approach learning very differently—each catering their efforts to match their learning style and preferences.

Bill Gates is now famous for his "reading weeks." Brian Grazer touts his curiosity conversations as the catalyst for his sustained success (see more on this in the chapter Talk with Strangers). I know a CEO who built a website thirty years ago in order to learn more about the then-emerging World Wide Web. I know another leader who has been listening to audiobooks religiously for more than twenty-five years. If someone followed you around for a day or two or looked at your calendar, what would they say about your commitment to lifelong learning?

Are You More Optimistic or Pessimistic?

The leader who can cast a fearful and pessimistic vision of the future and still attract a following is rare. One leader who made this work was explorer Ernest Shackleton. He supposedly posted this ad in his local paper while preparing for his famed expedition to Antarctica:

> *Men wanted for hazardous journey. Low wages, bitter cold, long hours of complete darkness. Safe return doubtful. Honor and recognition in event of success.*[5]

Today, people are most often attracted to leaders who believe in the possibility of a preferred future—a better future. We want leaders who can tell us where we are going and why it matters. Often, these same leaders will also address the consequences of inaction. These are the leaders people typically want to follow. To encourage is to give courage—pessimists rarely imbue others with courage.

Do You Assume Responsibility or Place Blame?

Most people like to be recognized and few like to be blamed. The best leaders fight both these tendencies—they are quick to accept responsibility and quick to give praise. When was the last time something you were responsible for went wrong? Hopefully, this doesn't happen often, but when it did, what did you do? If it happened on your watch, you are accountable and should accept responsibility. However, if things go extremely well, you should not be the one to accept the praise; give it to others.

You can see this difference play out on any given weekend in the fall just by watching the postgame interviews with the winning quarterbacks. Which of these two guys would you rather play for? "The coaches called a good game plan, the O line was outstanding, the receivers were unstoppable, and the defense was spectacular." Or the guy who says, "I was amazing today—I clearly brought my A game."

Are You a Courageous Leader?

Leadership requires action in massive doses. Action often requires courage. Therefore, courage is an indispensable part of leadership. So much of the role cannot be executed well without it. Hiring decisions, terminations, strategy decisions, budget allocations, placing a bet on an emerging leader or an unproven project, holding people and yourself accountable, standing up for what you believe in the face of opposition, and much more, all hinge on your willingness and ability to act courageously.

Would those who know you and work with you describe you as a courageous leader? If you need to increase your courage, here's one suggestion: make courageous decisions, even small ones. Courage is like a muscle: the more you use it, the stronger it becomes. Courage is the catalyst for outstanding leadership.

Are You a Serving Leader or a Self-Serving Leader?

As Ken Blanchard and I wrote twenty years ago, the best leaders are serving, not self-serving. I want to acknowledge the difficulty inherent in this statement. The ability to think of others first is not easy or natural. Most of us have been conditioned throughout our lifetimes to think about *ourselves* first; this is not the way of the servant leader. To think of others first is often countercultural, but it is my recommendation for anyone who wants to maximize their impact in this world.

One quick suggestion to combat the gravitational pull of selfishness: attempt to add value to everyone you meet. Now, before you point out the impossibility of this bit of advice, hold on. If my first priority is to add value to *you*, where is my focus? It is on you— not me. The effort and intent to add value transforms you. Even if you are unsuccessful in the moment, the effort will change you.

How Would Your Peers Describe Your Performance?

According to Peter Drucker, leadership can be assessed by two things: Do you have followers, and do you get results? Many of the preceding questions have addressed the follower part of Drucker's success criteria. Now, for the other side of the coin, how is your performance? And by *your*, I mean you personally and all of those people under your leadership. I often ask leaders about their performance. Sometimes I am surprised by their responses. If their first words are about external circumstances or disclaimers, it raises a yellow flag for me. There is at least a chance they are not taking full responsibility for their outcomes. Maybe a better question is the one above: How would your peers describe your performance?

How Would Your Supervisor Describe Your Performance?

You must have a good perspective on your own performance, but unless you are self-employed, you must also know how your boss views your performance. He or she will be a crucial voice regarding your future opportunities within your organization. You also need to understand some leaders are uncomfortable sharing the "last 10 percent." Let me explain.

Here's how a performance conversation might play out.

> **Supervisor:** "You are doing a really good job."
> **You:** "Anything else?" You are understandably curious because "really good" is not fantastic or outstanding.
> **Supervisor:** "No, nothing else."

If this is what you hear, I would suggest your leader is struggling to tell you the whole truth, including the last 10 percent. Consider a few "last 10 percent" prompts:

> **You:** "Thanks! What would I need to do so the next time we review my performance you would say, 'Amazing'?" Or "What specific suggestions do you have for me to improve my performance?"

What your supervisor thinks about your performance matters.

OWN YOUR STRENGTHS AND WEAKNESSES

As you worked through the assessment questions above, you may have come face to face with the reality that you are not gifted at everything. This is understandable. Counter to what many leaders want to believe, well-roundedness is a myth—at least at a high level. Perhaps it is easier to be well-rounded if you aren't very good at any facet of your role. Don't misinterpret what I am trying to say; you may not be excellent in every facet of your role, but this doesn't give you a pass on the need to improve. Before we talk about how to address the findings from the self-assessment questions, I want to encourage you to pull up and think more broadly about strengths and weaknesses.

How clear are you on your *real* strengths? If I handed you a three-by-five card and asked you to write your top strengths on the card, how long would it take? Now, since I've positioned this chapter to help leaders Confront Reality, here's a better question: If you handed out cards to ten people you work with—direct reports, peers, and others—and asked them to identify your top strengths, what would *they* say?

False positives are not a good thing. I once knew a leader who thought he had a specific strength that he didn't possess. He loved to talk, so he wanted to give speeches. The problem was that he wasn't a good communicator. Needless to say, this created issues. False positives surface outside of the workplace too. Think about the person who loves to sing in the shower and also wants to sing a solo in the choir. The only problem: that person can't sing.

Have you ever asked people to help you by affirming your strengths? If you are feeling courageous, you may want to give it a try.

The flip side of the same coin is also helpful. *Can you clearly and succinctly articulate your primary weaknesses?* Your response may be a by-product of the culture you work in. Some organizations are hyperfocused on helping people identify strengths. While others, probably less progressive, want to be absolutely sure every leader knows her or his weaknesses. I am in both camps. I want to know what others see as my strengths because these most likely represent my biggest opportunity to contribute. And I also want to know my weaknesses—some of them I can work on, others I will need to work around.

CLOSE GAPS AND SEIZE OPPORTUNITY

This is a critical point in your leadership story. Everyone loves to know about their strengths—it just feels good. When the subject shifts to weaknesses, however, we must move past our understandable discomfort and dig a little deeper.

There is a huge difference between a gap and an opportunity. The way I have thought about this for years is to disaggregate your current job into its four or five elemental or essential roles. As you assess each of these, you must be aware there is a baseline competency in each area. If one of your roles is coaching, you need to be able to coach people. If one of your roles is communications, you must demonstrate at least basic competency in this area.

Once these roles are clear, the next question follows: Is there a critical gap in any of these areas? I go back to my example of the young man who wanted to take on an additional project yet ranked thirty out of thirty in performance. Rather than focus on something new, a leader with a critical gap in a primary role should work to close that gap as soon as possible. These gaps, unaddressed, are career killers.

Assuming you have closed critical gaps, or none existed, you can then look at the core roles and decide which of them presents your best chance for impact. The opportunity can be based on organizational need or personal preference. The point is to be thoughtful. I would also suggest you have a conversation with your supervisor about your development. You would love to have his or her perspective, guidance, and support as you attempt to grow as a leader.

BUILD A BETTER VERSION OF YOU

Once you have a sense of where your best opportunities lie, or where gaps exist that you need to close, you will need a plan. Many leaders fail to grow not for lack of energy or desire. Instead, their shortcoming can often be boiled down to inadequate focus and accountability—a plan can help with both.

Over the years, I have resisted the temptation to give people a plan template. My reasons are a direct reflection of my own journey and my understanding that people are different. I never want the tool to become more important than the job the tool was meant to address. Therefore, rather than a template, I've chosen to share a few principles to help you create your own plan.

- **Write it down.** Written plans are exponentially better than plans that exist only in your head. Something magical happens when ideas leave your brain and show up on paper or on a computer screen. I don't understand it completely, but it is clarifying, more tangible, shareable, and more easily referenceable when it is written (or typed).

- **Focus your efforts.** We've covered much ground in this chapter and the previous one. Please don't try to boil the ocean. I've been looking at development plans for decades, and one of the most common mistakes I see is when people attempt to do too much. Pick a *few* areas to start with and make progress. You'll be glad you did.

- **Make it yours.** Your development plan should be *yours*— not anyone else's. If you learn better in the context of a relationship, find a mentor or a coach. If you are primarily an auditory learner, get a subscription to Audible. If you prefer a more detailed plan, make it detailed. If you want or need more room to explore, build that flexibility into *your* plan.

- **Be specific.** My life coach told me for years the only thing that happens when you are more specific is you accomplish more of your plan. He challenged me not to say, I'll work out three times per week; rather, I will work out at 6:30 a.m. on Monday, Wednesday, and Friday. He was right.

- **Track your progress.** This is the last, often difficult mile, and worth the effort. This is where you actually cross the finish line or score the touchdown. I'm looking for one more cliché… This is where the rubber meets the road. An outstanding plan is trash if you don't execute it. Tracking allows you to monitor your progress and make adjustments as needed.

- **Share your plan.** This is related to my previous idea about tracking. The goal of the plan is *not* to *have* a plan—it is to execute a plan that will facilitate your personal growth. If you share your plan with people who really care about you, it will help you with the get-it-done phase.

  One other advantage of the mastermind or other peer groups I mentioned earlier is having a ready group to share your annual plan with. My group has been doing this for more than twenty years—it helps me!

Whew! I know this chapter was a lot. However, if you make the Smart Choice to Confront Reality, you really should start with yourself. Regardless of how you fared during this look in the mirror, hang on—there are other Smart Choices to be made.

BE SMART!

Identify one strength and one weakness. Ask a few trusted voices to affirm or challenge your assessment. For now, I would suggest you not begin with your direct reports. What can you do to leverage the strength and strengthen your weakness? Write down your plans.

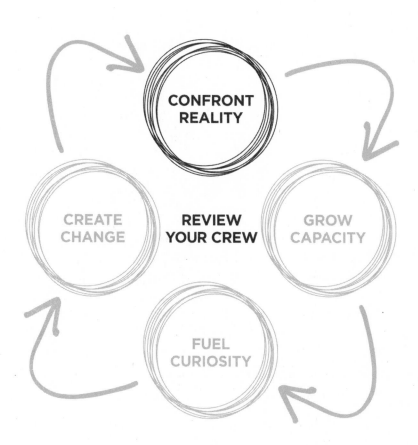

REVIEW YOUR CREW

"Your success will be determined by those closest to you."
John Maxwell

The year 1980 will likely be remembered for many things, such as the eruption of Mount St. Helens, the failed attempt to rescue American hostages from Iran, the debut of the Rubik's Cube, the fatal shooting of John Lennon, and the launch of CNN. But what may top the list for many is what *Sports Illustrated* called the Greatest Moment in Sports History.[1] A team of amateur hockey players from the United States beat the heavily favored defending gold medalists from the Soviet Union and went on to win Olympic gold. What most don't know, or remember, is some of the backstory that made this triumph virtually impossible.

The US team played a grueling sixty-one-game exhibition season in the months leading up to the Olympics. Their twenty-man roster was probably too young and inexperienced to know what lay before them. They were the youngest US team ever assembled, with an average age of twenty-two.

In their final pre-Olympic contest, they would face the Soviet team in Madison Square Garden. The Americans were embarrassed with a 10-3 defeat. No one was really surprised. The Soviets had won gold at the four previous Olympics and had won five of the last six—the last US win over them had been in 1960.

To cap it all off, the Americans were seeded seventh. Members of the US team understood; no one thought they had a chance. Some speculated they might finish as low as tenth in a field of twelve teams. No one in the world could imagine what the team was about to do, with one possible exception: the team's coach, Herb Brooks. Before the historic game, he told the team, "This is your time."

As it turned out, Brooks was correct. The US team demonstrated resilience, poise, and grit, coming from behind to defeat the Soviets 4-3. With this win under their belt, the US came from behind again to defeat Finland for gold. These young men emerged victorious—a modern-day David-versus-Goliath moment unfolded on a global stage. In doing so, they stirred the soul of an entire nation and captivated the world. Now, more than forty years later, this victory is still referred to as the "Miracle on Ice."

How does something like this happen? Yes, there was talent and outstanding coaching on the US side, while youth and energy probably played a role as well, but in the end, it was a sterling example of an outstanding team performance.

Other examples of men and women coming together to do something they could not have done alone abound in the world of sport and beyond. A team put men on the moon, landed a rover on Mars, and mapped the human genome. A team designed and built the world's tallest building, the Burj Khalifa, in Dubai, which stands at 2,716 feet.

We live in a team-based world and these examples remind us of the boundless potential available when talented women and men work together toward a common goal.

The world was once dominated by command-and-control organizational structures with little patience for the concept of teamwork. Those days are fading. According to the *Harvard Business Review*, the pace of collaborative work has increased by more than 50 percent in the last two decades.[2] A study from Deloitte a few years ago showed 53 percent of organizations moving to a team-based strategy saw "significant" performance improvements.[3] This is all good news on the surface; teams, when functioning well, do outperform individuals. However, based on my experience, few teams are living up to their full potential.

Some of my earliest childhood memories are from the baseball diamond. My parents signed me up to play at an early age. Although my memories are fuzzy, I clearly recall loving the experience. I remember in my middle school years, rolling around in the back of our station wagon changing uniforms while my mom drove me from one game to another. Clearly, this was in the days before seat belts. These back seat gymnastics were necessary because I was playing on two different teams at the same time.

As I reflect on those days, I played in hundreds of baseball games with few trophies to show for it. But this lack of "success" didn't diminish my enthusiasm; it did, however, increase my awareness—most of the teams I was on were not good, and at the time, I had no idea why.

Fast-forward a couple of decades, and total quality management was all the rage in Japan. I was leading our quality efforts at the time, when I was charged by our company president to help us become a team-based organization. He knew teams would be required to manage the growing complexity we faced and capitalize on the opportunities of the future. He was right. His vision launched a journey of more than two decades to discover why some teams flourished while others, like my childhood teams, floundered.

What our research ultimately revealed is the best teams, the extraordinary ones, have a few things in common. One, they don't just happen. Great teams are the product of leadership, strategic intent, and thoughtful design. No team drifts to greatness—they are built for success.

EVALUATE YOUR TEAM

The elite teams—we call them High Performance Teams—also have some other elements in common. I've written about this in greater depth in a book entitled *The Secret of Teams*. But in the context of this work, I want to help you evaluate your current team with seven simple questions. There is much more for you to explore, but these questions should be sufficient to help you take the next steps on your journey. You cannot fully Confront Reality without looking at your team.

Do You Have the Right People on Your Team?

Talent matters. There's a blinding flash of the obvious. But before we dismiss this as just another cliché, let's think about it in terms of the women and men sitting around your leadership table.

I had the privilege a few years ago to coach a young and talented leader who wanted to improve the performance of his business. After several conversations, he said he wanted to focus on improving his leadership team. Based on what I had learned about his situation, this appeared to be a good place for him to start.

After a few more conversations, and honestly some frustration on his part, he announced to me that he had figured out his problem. I waited with much anticipation. He said, "I don't have the right people around the table."

I said, "Fantastic!"

I think he wanted to strangle me. He immediately wanted me to defend my response. I told him, "Now you can build a plan to solve the problem." Prior to his revelation, he had no idea why his business was not performing up to his expectations—now he knew.

I've worked with leaders from around the world who have never been able to find such clarity on this critical issue. I'll repeat the quote from John Maxwell at the beginning of this chapter: "Your success will be determined by those closest to you." Do you have the right people on your leadership team?

I cannot answer that question for you, but I can give you a few additional questions to help you evaluate your team members.

- *If you needed to make a long-term strategic decision that would impact your organization for years to come, who are the five to seven people from your organization you would want around the table?* Are these the same people who currently sit on your leadership team? Maybe they should be.

- *Does your team reflect a high level of diversity?* I'm not just talking about race and gender, which are both important, but do you also have different functional responsibilities, backgrounds, personalities, education, and so on represented? If you are not careful and strategic, you may fall into the trap of attracting people just like you. This might be good for a bowling team, but it's a lousy idea for a leadership team. A baseball team with nine second basemen is destined to be a perennial underperformer.

- *Can the women and men on your team help your organization go where it needs to go?* This is perhaps the most difficult question of all. Obviously, your team members were capable enough to get you where you are today. The more gut-wrenching and soul-searching question: *Do they have the capabilities and the personal capacity to create the future?*

  One of the best leaders I know told me the most difficult decisions he's ever had to make were those when he had to remove someone from his team, not for poor past performance but for lack of future potential. They did not have the capacity to lead at the *next* level.

Does Every Member Fully Embrace Your Organization's and Team's Purpose?

The power of a strong and clear personal sense of purpose is undeniable. However, this same power is often overlooked when it comes to a team.

I saw this played out recently with my granddaughter, Addie. Now, I want to acknowledge she was barely three at the time, but upon arriving at her first soccer game, no one explained to her, and as far as I know, to any of the children, that the objective was to kick the ball into the net. The only thing that saved the day was a few of the older children who had obviously played before. For Addie and most of the kids, soccer was about running aimlessly, snacks, and crying because the other children wouldn't let them kick the ball.

Have you ever been on a team that was unclear on its purpose? One in which the team thought the purpose was running around aimlessly and snacks? Hopefully, there was no crying. Far too many of the teams I've encountered during my career are not aligned on their purposes, objectives, or key deliverables. I know this may sound crazy. Tragically, I've seen it countless times.

I had been invited by a large, well-established nonprofit organization to meet with their senior leadership team. As I recall, their request had been rather vague, but I thought I would show up, listen, learn, and help if I could. As with virtually every consulting effort, I began with some questions. It became apparent to me rather quickly the group was not aligned on what the organization was trying to accomplish.

I asked a few more questions, trying to confirm my suspicions. At that point, the senior leader figured out where I was headed. He said something to the effect of, "We've been doing this work for over a hundred years."

I said, "I'm not questioning your longevity; I'm questioning your clarity."

Since he didn't throw me out of the room, I handed out three-by-five cards and asked each member of the team to answer one question: "Why does your organization exist?"

After a few minutes, I collected the cards and began to read them. The first was brilliant, the language compelling and, honestly, inspiring. I read the second—it was equally well-written, yet it was different. I continued to read the third, fourth, and fifth cards. I stopped only after I had read a dozen cards. They were all different. Each member was thoughtful and sincere with a real heart to serve the organization. But leadership had failed to articulate a clear, compelling, and unifying purpose.

If you are not aligned on what the organization is trying to accomplish, it is exceedingly difficult to be aligned on what your team is supposed to do. Clarity on both of these issues is critical.

Does Your Team Have Shared Goals?

Simply stated, the best teams have goals, often very aggressive ones. I've been studying High Performance Teams for over thirty years. I cannot remember one example in which these teams did not have at least one compelling goal. Often, they had more than one. However, because I've encountered so many teams desiring high performance that have missed this fundamental truth, I want to slow down and share several reasons goals matter—this is a partial list.

- **Goals unify a team.** When does a team become a team? I've given this a lot of thought over the years. I don't think it's on draft day or day one of training camp. Nor is it when the team gets its first win or suffers its first crushing defeat. A team becomes a team when they embrace a common goal(s).

- **Goals clarify priorities.** Once a goal or goals are established, priorities can be set. In the absence of goals, how is a team to know what matters most? Everything can't be equally important nor should it. A team needs all the help they can get sorting through multiple priorities—goals help.

- **Goals drive strategies.** If the team decides the goal is a 5 percent increase over the previous year, that conjures up any number of possible strategies. However, if the same team sets a goal to increase by 25 percent, a totally different set of strategies will likely be required. Different activities drive different results. Strategies can only be thoughtfully established in service of a goal.

- **Goals affect resource allocation.** This may be too obvious to discuss. When a team or an organization sets a goal, in virtually all cases, resources will be required to achieve the goal. These resources can be time, money, energy, or people. Most often, the bigger the goal, the more resources will be required. An unresourced goal is not a legitimate goal.

- **Goals should impact structure.** Structure should enable the accomplishment of work—not hinder it. If you have goals regarding international expansion, new product development, or increased domestic market share, you will increase your odds of success if you build structure around the pursuit of those goals. Structural changes alone can often make the impossible inevitable.

- **Goals improve performance.** There is much written about the power of goals. Whether in sports, business, or your personal finances, women, men, young people, athletes, businesspeople, and teams that set and pursue goals outperform those who do not. Goals are a powerful lever in the leader's toolbox.

Does Your Team Have Absolute Role Clarity?

I remember a brief encounter with a leader about his team. I could tell by his tone he was frustrated. As I recall the conversation, it went something like this:

> **Leader:** I'm having issues with my team.
>
> **Me:** Sorry you're having challenges. What do you think the problem is?
>
> **Leader:** My leaders are not solving problems.
>
> **Me:** Why?
>
> **Leader:** I don't know. That's what I want you to tell me.
>
> **Me:** Can you give me an example?
>
> **Leader:** Sure. It happened again yesterday. I walked in and found a problem no one was addressing.
>
> **Me:** What did you do?
>
> **Leader:** I solved it.
>
> **Me:** Okay, based on this very short consulting intervention, let me take a guess at the root problem here. I think you have a role-clarity issue here. You've asked your leaders to solve problems, but they don't believe you really want their help.
>
> **Leader:** Why don't they believe me?
>
> **Me:** Because of your willingness to jump in and solve the problem, they have never accepted that as part of *their* role.

This is just one example showing how lack of role clarity can hamper a team's effectiveness.

If you are the leader, you can decide the role you want to play and the role you want your team to play. *But you need to decide.* Here are a few ideas to jump-start your thinking:

The Leader's Role	The Leadership Team's Role
• *Provide vision*	• *Communicate vision*
• *Establish values*	• *Enforce the core values*
• *Set goals*	• *Manage the day-to-day activities*
• *Endorse core strategies*	• *Identify and solve problems*
• *Provide resources*	• *Lift and maintain engagement*
• *Provide encouragement*	• *Train and equip team members*
• *Invest in leaders*	• *Develop next generation leaders*
• *Establish boundaries*	• *Provide accountability*
• *Clarify roles*	• *Improve performance*

Don't miss the big idea here—regardless of who does what, be *clear* and explicit. The absence of role clarity is not a team failure—it is a leadership failure.

Does Your Team Invest Time Strategically Building Community?

After several decades of studying teams, we were still struggling to connect the dots. We knew there were at least four types of teams:

- Pseudo-Teams
- Mediocre Teams
- Good Teams
- Outstanding Teams (We later called these High Performance Teams.)

Even with the different team types identified, we were having trouble deciphering the elemental components of each one. It was easy to figure out what the pseudo-teams and mediocre teams had in common—invariably, the problem was a lack of leadership and skills. The trick was discerning and articulating the difference between the good teams and the outstanding teams (High Performance Teams). After years of investigation, we finally found the answer. Good teams have talent and skills. What sets High Performance Teams apart is that they add a third element—we call it *community*.

Let's focus on this idea of community as you evaluate your team. Community is the turbocharger (and the missing element) many of you have been looking for, and it has four primary characteristics.

- **People know each other deeply.** It is uncanny how many women and men work side by side with others and know little about one another as human beings. I have witnessed this many times. What are the personal passions of the people on your team? What do they do when they are not at work? What are their hopes and dreams? What do you know about their families? Their hobbies? Their pasts? All of this is knowable. And although some of these items in isolation may feel trivial, community is cumulative—we build it piece by piece, slowly revealing a complicated, nuanced, and beautiful, three-dimensional puzzle that is their life. As leaders, we can facilitate these conversations to ensure our team members know each other deeply.

- **People serve each other unconditionally.** Lou Holtz, the former coach of the Notre Dame Fighting Irish and the South Carolina Gamecocks, was a huge fan of community, although he didn't have a name for it when he promoted this type of connection within his teams. I had the opportunity to talk with him about his approach and the various tactics he employed. One of them was to normalize serving others on the team. He told me he often ended practice by calling the team together and asking if anyone needed help with anything. Sometimes a player would need a ride, and they would figure out who could make it happen. Sometimes a player would say, "I have a math test tomorrow." Coach would ask, "Who can do math?" and everyone would laugh. Then they would try to figure out who could provide assistance. He said he did this over and over again. When you serve one another off the field, wonderful things happen on the field. Leaders can model this servant spirit, encourage it, and facilitate it.

- **People celebrate and mourn authentically.** If you had great news to share or a personal tragedy to report, who would you call? One of the cornerstones of community is the gift of presence—just being with someone when life is full of joy or full of sorrow. This element of community can manifest itself in big events and small, like a teammate graduating college or adopting a puppy. The question is not, "What would I celebrate?" In community, the better question is, "What would my teammate celebrate?" Go there with them.

  I remember going to a coworker's son's first middle school football game. Not because this was a big deal to me—because it was a big deal to him. I have also attended many weddings and funerals over the years because I have chosen to live in community.

- **People genuinely love one another.** This is probably going to be the squishiest thing you'll hear me advocate in this entire book, but stay with me. There are countless appropriate ways to express gratitude, appreciation, thanks, and love. Random acts of kindness, notes of thanks and appreciation, unsolicited acts of service, and more come to memory as I think about communities I have been a part of over the years.

  If you create a place where people know, serve, celebrate, and mourn together consistently, over time, love and the appreciation of others in the circle will be a natural outcome of your efforts. People are starved for genuine community. Some find this community in more traditional places like family, schools, churches, or clubs. The best teams, the high-performance ones, create these transformational conditions in the workplace. Wherever community exists, people thrive. Love is still perhaps the most powerful motivator in the universe. Some teams have chosen to tap into that power. You can too.

Community, like I just described, rarely, if ever, occurs spontaneously. I was talking with John Katzenbach, the coauthor of *The Wisdom of Teams*, about this phenomenon. He too had seen the power of community, although he described it as a by-product of genuine care and concern and didn't have a name for it. He said, based on his research, if someone worked in a team-based organization their entire career, they would likely only encounter this type of team *once in a lifetime.*

I told him I could probably agree with him on the low probability if left to chance. However, if a leader embraces community as the third element of his or her strategy for high performance, along with talent and skills, I think you can achieve it almost every time.

In summary, community is a place where people do life together. Does this sound like your team?

Does Your Team Have Effective Meetings Focused on Performance Improvement?

Let's be honest: most meetings are awful. They waste time, energy, emotions, opportunity, and money. However, the best teams have amazing meetings.

Have you ever stopped to think about why most meetings are not worth the effort? It's not because the practices of effective meetings are unknown; it's not that the process is particularly challenging; it's not because leaders are not smart enough to create good meetings. It is largely a failure of vision. That's right—vision. Most leaders undervalue the huge potential of their meetings. A leader's limited vision will always become the team's reality.

Years ago, I was leading a group of volunteers in a large nonprofit organization. When I introduced them to my concept of meetings, their initial reaction was predictable—they pushed back, probably for the same reason you would, because their past experiences with meetings were terrible.

Then, I began to cast vision for what our monthly meetings would be. It went something like this:

Imagine a time and place each month in which you are challenged, equipped, celebrated; problems are solved, and encouragement is available in generous supply. You are held accountable to bring your best, your vision is expanded, you build lifelong relationships of genuine care and concern, and collectively, you make a huge impact on the world. Anyone interested in being part of something like that?

They were intrigued but skeptical. It sounded too good to be true. And then, I put the cherry on the top by saying, "My goal is that our meeting would be the highlight of your month."

Absurd? Maybe, maybe not. How good do you want your meetings to be? Really.

I knew we had made progress when after several months someone told me they had changed their vacation plans so they wouldn't have to miss a meeting!

Cast a bold vision for the power and potential of your meetings—they will never rise above your ambition.

Does Your Team Have a Scorecard to Guide Their Actions?

High Performance Teams keep score. They are focused on achieving some predetermined result. To me, this is one of the most obvious and yet most often overlooked indicators of a healthy team. If you've ever played sports, or even watched sports, it's probably hard for you to fathom a serious team not keeping score. I used to say, when a team isn't keeping score, they're just practicing. Then, I began to realize the best teams even keep score in practice.

During several interviews focused on execution, I learned it is not uncommon for Division I football teams to grade every player's execution on every play in every *practice*. I also discovered this same discipline during a conversation with a leader from an NFL team. In his case, the players receive daily scorecards on their actual execution—play by play.

We were interviewing the head of ground operations for a major US airline, who told us about a "breakthrough" his organization experienced a few years ago. They moved from forty-three key metrics to eight. I agreed this sounded like progress but pressed him a little and said I thought eight was still a lot. He agreed and then revealed they only have three *primary* outcome metrics and five key drivers—for a total of eight numbers on their scorecard. He went on to say that every team member reviews those critical numbers every day.

How often does your team look at its scorecard? When they do, is it focused on the critical few metrics that drive performance?

HOW DID YOUR TEAM NET OUT?

How strong is your team? Here is the best news you'll probably receive today: regardless of how you rated your team today, you can create a different future. The *current* status of your team can become nothing more than a footnote in history as you continue to raise their future contribution and performance. You do have to start where you are, but you do not have to stay there. More on this in our next Smart Choice!

BE SMART!

Conduct a High Performance Team Assessment. Use the previous questions, create your own, or download a more robust evaluation for *free* at SmartLeadershipBook.com/Team.

GROW
CAPACITY

GROW CAPACITY

*"There is no man living who isn't capable
of doing more than he thinks he can do."*
Henry Ford

The quest for capacity predates recorded history. Just imagine the sheer joy when the first wheel was invented—probably 5,500 years ago. Historians believe the first wheels were not used for transportation; they were potter's wheels. It would be another three hundred years before the wheel was used on chariots. This leap to transportation made things possible that were previously impossible. That's the way capacity-building endeavors impact our world to this day—they make the impossible possible.

The same can be said for Henry Ford's 1908 Model T. It created unprecedented mobility for people and products. The greater capacity breakthrough was the introduction of the assembly line in 1913. This manufacturing approach took the time required to produce a car from twelve hours to one hour and thirty-three minutes. From 1913 to 1927, Ford produced over fifteen million Model Ts.[2]

In our modern world, the computer has created incomprehensible levels of capacity. And like many other capacity-building innovations, computers have enabled previously unimagined activities such as the sequencing of the human genome to be completed with ease. As of this writing, the fastest supercomputer is Fugaku in Japan. It boasts nearly 7.3 million cores and a speed of 415.5 peta-flops.[3] I have no idea how fast that is. But the capacity it creates, like many other innovations, will change our world.

Leaders easily grasp the impact and implications of technology and invention on capacity. The best leaders also understand there is a softer side to the issue of capacity—the human side.

Human beings have infinite capacity to explore, discover, inno-vate, and create. Where did all of the breakthroughs in history come from? The minds of women and men who were not satisfied with the status quo. There is tremendous untapped potential in the heads, hearts, hands, and imaginations of the people we lead. As the archi-tects of the future, we have the unspeakable opportunity to release that potential. When we do, people and organizations flourish.

THE SMART CHOICE

Grow Capacity to meet the demands of the moment and the challenges of the future.

As in previous chapters, I'll provide some macro suggestions, and then we'll do a deep dive on two specific practices in the chapters that follow.

By now, you should begin to see the interconnectedness of the four Smart Choices. If you do not first make the choice to Confront Reality, you will most likely never muster the confidence or develop the urgency required to Grow Capacity. This audacious belief that your capacity and the capacity of your team is not fixed is central to your growing influence and impact as a leader. If you do not decide to Grow Capacity, it will not spontaneously appear. The choice pre-cedes the capacity.

Start with Yourself

When you consider the topic of capacity, it may be tempting to look at your team and see their gaps, weaknesses, and opportunities. The capacity of your team is a valid concern; that's why we devoted an entire chapter to evaluating your team. However, the place to start your quest for capacity is not out there; you must begin by growing your personal capacity. Growing leaders grow organizations. If successful, your newfound capacity can become the catalyst for increasing team and organizational capacity. This should become clearer as we go along.

Clarify Your Role

This may sound strange, but don't move on too quickly. I have met many leaders who have lost a grip on this issue. One of several things happened at some point in their career:

- They never had clarity regarding what their role should be in the first place.
- The quicksand we discussed previously sucked them into survival mode and they went from being the captain of the ship to manning the lifeboats.
- As their organization grew, they failed to adjust their priorities accordingly.
- They haven't performed their role well in the past, which has created today's gaps.
- Their supervisors have recognized them for the wrong behaviors.
- Some combination of the above.

I do want to offer one cautionary note as we consider your role: it is never your job to do the team's job. If you are willing to do their job, they will likely let you. If you are doing their job, chances are you will not have sufficient capacity remaining to do *your* job. Moving work to its rightful owner is a tremendous way for many leaders to instantly grow their capacity. Bill Belichick, coach of the New England Patriots, has become famous for exhorting his team members to "Do your job."⁴ This is good advice for leaders too.

Clean Up Your Calendar

I was tempted to do an entire chapter on this topic but instead decided to just remind you of one basic idea:

Your time is your life.

The seconds, minutes, hours, days, weeks, months, and years chronicled in your daily calendar are the building blocks of your impact and legacy. The Smart Choice to Grow Capacity is a game changer for virtually every leader. As you activate this choice, you will have _more time_ to strategically invest in the impact you want to make on the world.

There are scores of books on the topic of personal productivity written by women and men who have devoted their careers to helping you manage the details of your life and leadership. If this is an area where you struggle, seek out those experts.

As a lifelong student of personal productivity, I do have three ideas regarding your calendar that continue to serve me well.

- **Eliminate.** Much of what most leaders do does not add significant strategic value. I know that sounds harsh, but it's true. This isn't to say your intentions aren't good. What I am saying is many of the activities on our calendars don't help us do our jobs any better; they don't enhance performance and they do not align with our stated priorities.

  Peter Drucker said years ago that he had never met a "knowledge worker" who could not eliminate 25 percent of the items from his calendar and no one would notice.⁵

  As Drucker defined the term, you and I are knowledge workers. We think for a living; we invest much of our time solving complex problems; we create products and services;

we have a relatively high degree of autonomy regarding our work process; and our days are filled with nonroutine tasks. I wonder what percentage of our activities we could eliminate.

One way to eliminate low or non-value-added activities is the qualified yes. In this way, you're not completely eliminating tasks but making them more manageable. When you are invited to an all-day meeting, ask to see the agenda in advance. If you have sufficient liberty, ask the person who invited you, "Which portion of the meeting would be most helpful for me to attend?" Their answer may be only a portion of the full day. If that is the case, only attend the portion they suggest.

Try this exercise: look back at your calendar for the last month. Evaluate the activities recorded there based on your contribution. A simple red (for those to stop doing), yellow (for those you're unsure about), or green (for those you want to keep doing) will be sufficient. Now, do the same activity for the upcoming month. Flag those activities and events where you have concerns about the value you will add. Work diligently to eliminate the red ones for sure; more investigation may be required for the yellow ones. Maybe selective or partial participation is the right path.

- **Chunk.** I know a leader's time is not his or her own. Depending on your role and responsibilities, you have many competing demands for your time. I also know many of these are out of your control from a timing standpoint. Nonetheless, our calendar is a tool, which if used wisely can create more capacity. One strategy is chunking. It's not new and many authors and experts have written about its power.

    Here is the concept in a nutshell—cluster or chunk like activities. The more you can do this, the more you can lessen the switching costs. These are the physical and mental taxes you pay when you move from one activity to another.

Let's start with a tangible example. If you are in an organization with multiple buildings, can you schedule meetings back-to-back in one building as opposed to going from building to building between meetings? How about the way you schedule your off-site appointments? When I plan a trip to the West Coast, I chunk or cluster meetings up and down the West Coast to save on the switching costs of flying across the country multiple times. Can you chunk your meetings on a certain day or days of the week? Can you chunk your meetings in the morning or afternoon versus spreading them out across the entire day? How about dedicating a chunk of time periodically for email and other administrative tasks? These tactical examples create space on your calendar (aka capacity).

- **Track.** If you want to clean up your calendar and do your job, some personal accountability will probably be helpful. Tracking where you invest your time is a valuable discipline. Admittedly, early in my career, I would occasionally track my time for a season—a week or two. I should have been smarter. The only thing I remember from those random experiments is I learned something every time I did it. The big takeaway: I was never using my time as I thought I was.

  These days, I track all my working time. Beyond that, I have goals for how I will use my time and look at a monthly and year-to-date report for personal accountability and to make any needed adjustments. A quick administrative note: this is not as hard as it might sound. If you color code tasks on your calendar, reports can be generated at will. If that doesn't work for you, there are dozens of apps designed to help you track your time.

Leverage Technology

Although I want to focus your attention on the untapped human capacity resident in all of us, we should not ignore technology.

Technology and the tools that embody it can significantly increase your capacity. Wise leaders understand this.

One of the silver linings of working during the COVID crisis has been the forced reliance on virtual meetings. I know video-based meetings will never replace face-to-face meetings, but this technology gives leaders another tool for their toolbox. In the future, I'm guessing trillions of dollars of capacity will be freed up as leaders think twice about how they steward their time in light of present technology and recent experience. One leader I talked to recently said the days of him flying across the country for a two-hour meeting are over. He will not be the only one leveraging technology to grow personal and organizational capacity.

Create Margin

What is margin? Broadly defined, margin is what appears to be excess time, space, and capacity—time free of normal activities and demands. In reality, margin is not excess; it is essential for Smart Leaders. As it turns out, the magic is not the time alone—it's what these leaders do with the time.

The idea of creating margin as a means of growing capacity was one of our team's biggest insights from the last couple of years. Admittedly, carving out margin in our lives and leadership is not only countercultural but also counterintuitive. To a leader swimming in quicksand, the mere suggestion he or she should have margin in their schedule sounds crazy.

Imagine a book with the words running off the edges of the pages. Now, look at the calendars of many leaders, and you'll see they are overstuffing their days and eliminating any white space on the pages of their lives. The consequence is a life that is hard to live— exhaustion has replaced exhilaration.

A call for margin is a call for sobriety; for many leaders, our addiction is activity. Margin is the gateway to freedom. Only there will we find the time and space to clear our minds, step out of the fray, and think carefully about the role we have been asked to play and the world we are trying to create. To embrace this practice requires leaders to jettison the notion that activity equals accomplishment and busyness is the same as effectiveness.

Margin is simply the practice of allocating enough time to reflect, assess, think, create, and plan. We *must* create sufficient capacity for this critical work. Our leadership depends on it. Without margin in our life, we run the very real risk of unwittingly sacrificing the future on the altar of today.

Margin as a personal discipline for leaders is not a new idea. The practice can be traced back at least to the first century. More recently, Howard Gardner saw this pattern of behavior emerge in the extraordinary leaders he studied for his book *Leading Minds*, including Churchill, Einstein, Margret Mead, Gandhi, General George Marshall, Margaret Thatcher, Martin Luther King Jr., and more. He described their practice as a *rhythm of life*, consisting of periods of immersion and isolation.[6] Isolation provides the insight.

Few leaders I know shy away from the immersion, the day-to-day activities. However, these are exactly the tasks, obligations, and distractions that create their own gravitational pull—a pull away from our future toward our present. We cannot usher in a better future unless we invest the time to envision and prepare for it. We'll go deeper on margin in the chapter Stop and Think.

Take Care of Yourself

We are all human, and with our humanity comes some limits. If you have been a leader for a while, I'm sure you have encountered situations in which your personal capacity was the limiting factor preventing further progress. The root problem was probably not your desire, or competence, but that you just didn't have the physical or emotional energy to meet the demands of the moment.

Even though it is appropriate to acknowledge our limits as leaders, we should not see these boundaries as fixed. If you and I will take care of our physical bodies, we can create more energy. More on this in the chapter Expand Your Energy.

For now, I want you to imagine your leadership if you had 10, 20, 30 percent more energy. What could you accomplish? How would your newfound energy impact your thinking, your decisions, and your relationships? Tragically, I have known leaders who knew how to lead; they just didn't have the energy to do it well. You do not have to be one of those leaders. If this promise sounds too good to be true, stay with me for a few more chapters.

Design for Scale

A few years ago, I heard a talk by T. D. Jakes. Some of you may know that name, and others may not. That's okay. Here's the context. Jakes is the pastor of a very large church, has a television show, produces motion pictures, owns a record label, is an author and speaker, and has several other business holdings. During an interview, he was asked how he managed to give his best effort to so many different ventures. Here is the gist of what he said: *If a leader is in a sustained period of stress and pressure, he or she doesn't have the proper structure. Structure, by design, is supposed to lift and support. A lot of leaders are trying to carry too much; they are shouldering weight beyond what they were intended to carry—they need a different structure.*[7]

You may want to read that again. If the pressure is sustained, the structure could be a significant contributor; Jakes would say it is *the* problem. His operating premise is he can continue to add weight and additional responsibilities because he created a structure that can support the work.

We see this same principle play out all around us as we consider large conglomerates. Many of their CEOs effectively lead dozens of companies. The enabler: the appropriate structure. Why should we allow this insight to only serve multinational CEOs? The right structure can lighten the load for virtually every leader.

The purpose of structure, according to Jakes, is to lift and support. I would add to that the idea that structure should also facilitate efficient and effective execution of the task at hand. The word facilitate means to make easier. Does your structure make it easier to do the work? Does your structure enable efficient and effective execution? Creating an organizational structure to accomplish these simple objectives is another facet of our role as leaders that is much easier to talk about than it is to do.

How do you know if structure presents an opportunity you should address? Here are a few questions based on the premise that structure should make it easier to handle the pressure and help you and others do the work required.

- Is it really hard to get the work done—harder than you think it should be?
- Is the flow of information slow, confusing, or nonexistent?
- Is performance slipping? (Granted, there are many factors that contribute to performance. However, don't overlook structure as a potential root cause.)
- Are problems viewed as coming from "over there" (another individual, team, or department)?

My final counsel regarding structure is to always hold it loosely. I know a gifted leader who stands before his leadership team every year and, referring to the blank flip chart, says, "This is our structure for the upcoming year."

The first time he did this, one of his team members hesitantly said, "Boss, it's blank."

His response, "I know, and it's our job to figure out how we should be structured to best serve our team and our customers over the next year."

I'm not suggesting you redesign your organization's structure every year. What I am suggesting is you should be *willing* to do so if necessary. Too often, we assume the role of victim, living in an outdated structure, pretending there's nothing we can do about it. I have known leaders who let an old structure prevent them from realizing their dreams. My answer is always evaluate your structure and change it when needed.

Designing for scale certainly includes structure, but it is much bigger. You must also consider your mindset and beliefs about your highest contribution to the organization and design your role accordingly. And finally, you need a strategy to enroll every member of your organization—this is the ultimate competitive advantage and the fast track to scale.

WHAT'S YOUR ROLE?

Years ago, I was introduced to what I think of as the typical life cycle of a growing leader. The story often goes something like this:

Doer

Early in their career, most would-be leaders are primarily doers. This behavior can manifest itself in several ways. Perhaps the future leader is only an individual contributor with leadership potential. This person makes his or her reputation for getting things done. Other times, a leader may actually be in a position of leadership, but he or she primarily functions as a doer. These are often the leaders who confess, "I'm too busy to lead." And in many situations, the leader, regardless of role and responsibility, maintains the limiting mindset and role of a doer.

Delegator

Then one day, as a by-product of insight, revelation, coaching, frustration, or perhaps exhaustion, the doer discovers delega-tion. It is a glorious moment for a leader to realize others can help do the work. This is on one level liberating and on another level imprisoning. The core problem with delegation is the need for the leader to be the delegator. I've talked to leaders who feel like a prisoner of their business. If they are not physically present to identify what needs to be done and delegate the work, it doesn't happen.

Developer

When leaders get stuck in delegation mode, it is a tragedy. However, many do discover they can grow, mature, and progress to the developer stage of their careers. This is where the fun really begins. The focus shifts from tasks to people. This phase results in leaders narrowing their focus and often finding themselves investing heavily in key leaders. This is not a bad place to be, but if not careful, leaders can get stuck here just as with the previous phases. What does a leader do when other leaders have already been developed? If you are willing, you can advance one more level.

Designer

Doer, delegator, developer, and finally, designer. This is where the design for scale idea really comes to life. A leader in this final stage can leverage all he or she has learned on their leadership journey to see the big picture, envision a preferred future, identify gaps and opportunities, and build an organization capable of making the vision a reality. Leaders willingly embrace their role as they design the vision, culture, structure, system, and strategy for the organization. Make no mistake, little of this design work is a solo effort. Teams of talented people contribute widely for the design to move from conceptual to concrete.

Organizations that scale well are designed to scale. Those that scale without thoughtful design leave untold untapped potential on the table. The costs for the lost human potential, creativity, innovation, and what could have been, cannot be calculated. Left to the natural course of events, organizations evolve or devolve. The ethos in these "organic" organizations is often marked by inefficiency, waste, and lethargy rather than innovation, engagement, and increasing impact.

Avoiding these maladies is possible. Leaders can, with strategic intent, build an organization that maximizes performance while valuing the individuals involved. This only occurs when leaders serve as the chief designers and become a catalytic force in the process.

One more thought about the four phases: doer, delegator, developer, and designer. Mature leaders understand these are not rigid categories nor are they mutually exclusive. There will be times when every leader willingly, and without prompting, moves from one role to another. This is not a problem, but often a necessary contribution. The problem occurs when a leader becomes stuck in any of the first three roles for a prolonged period of time. If you allow this to happen, you forfeit the opportunity for a higher level of contribution—and impact.

WHAT'S THE CATCH?

The potential of an ever-expanding future with unparalleled growth, opportunity, and capacity probably sounds good to most of you. So what's the catch? The catch is that leaders must lead the way. Our future success is not predestined nor guaranteed. You and I are most often the bottleneck. The quest for capacity must begin with us.

Some may wonder, "Is there really untapped potential and unrealized capacity out there in the universe to be harnessed?" This skepticism is one of several obstacles leaders must overcome. If you cannot overcome your own disbelief, your pessimism will be rewarded, and the increased capacity I am referring to will never manifest itself under your leadership. However, assuming you can see it, here are a few other stumbling blocks to look out for.

Fear of Change

Fear is a natural human emotion; leaders are not immune. But courage is the willingness to act even in the face of fear. If allowed, fear will limit your impact, blind you to a preferred future, and wreck your leadership. You will not grow capacity, personally or in your organization, without change. Hope is not a strategy. You must be willing to change. Change is *not* the enemy; change is your job. We must find the courage to move forward. Leadership is about helping people and organizations move into the unknown with confidence. This confidence is a reflection of leadership.

Management versus Leadership Mindset

Management and leadership are both required for an organization to succeed. However, the role of the manager and leader are different. A manager's responsibility is generally focused on control while a leader is focused on growth. Managers are focused on today whereas leaders are primarily concerned with tomorrow. Granted, I've met very few pure managers or pure leaders—most of us are a blend. To be crystal clear, I'll repeat myself: successful organizations *require* both management and leadership. But it is important to understand the different roles, your personal tendencies, and how to ensure you use these two skill sets appropriately. It is very easy for a management mindset to create a shortsightedness that will derail your efforts to grow long-lasting capacity.

Inertia

This is one of the few concepts of physics I remember from my formative years of education. I think it may have been the way the teacher helped me visualize the idea. As I recall my moment of clarity, the teacher took a small card, about one inch square, and a small wooden block, balanced the card on my upturned finger, and then placed the block in the center of the card. Without notice, she flipped the card out from under the block, and it remained perched on my finger. She said the reason the block didn't move is something we call inertia—an object at rest will remain at rest until acted upon by some outside force. The movement of the card produced no force on the block, so the block just sat there.

I think this simple illustration is why many leaders don't focus their energy on growing capacity—they are at rest. Things are good, or at least tolerable, and there is no apparent outside force stirring them to action. Another word for this is *complacency*.

You may have heard this compelling outside force described as a "burning platform." Yes, when one exists, a clear and present danger can serve as a catalyst for change, but fear-based leadership is hard to maintain. "Change or die" can only work for so long. Future-oriented, vision-based leadership is much more sustainable.

———

I was challenged recently by John Mark Comer's book *The Ruthless Elimination of Hurry*. One of my personal insights was that it's fine to be busy, but hurry is the enemy. Busy is about our calendars; hurry is about our hearts. One of the surefire ways to find the thin space between the two is to Grow Capacity. This choice will not only help with your calendar, but you may also find it life-giving and soul-enriching. Don't be surprised if with your newfound capacity you also receive a bonus: renewed passion and higher levels of personal energy.

The Smart Choice to Grow Capacity is similar to the other Smart Choices in that you must make it over and over again. The quicksand will always be there beckoning you. One false step and you can find yourself sucked back in. Grow Capacity is one of the four choices for a reason—without ample capacity, you will never make it to higher ground.

BE SMART!

Although there are many strategies and tactics to Grow Capacity, the most straightforward is to eliminate activities from your calendar. Here's my challenge to you: look at your calendar for the upcoming month and remove at least one meeting or activity per week. If successful, you will be better prepared for the ideas in the next chapter.

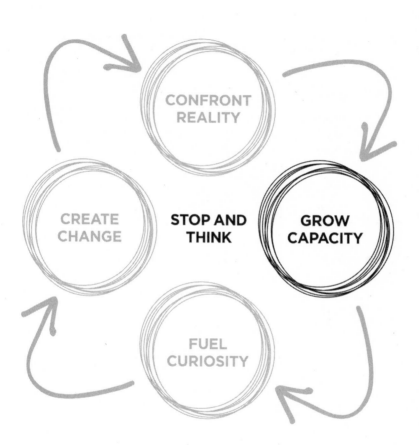

STOP AND THINK

"Public victory is always preceded by private victory."
Stephen Covey

I attended a conference a few years ago themed around the idea of liminal space. This was a new concept for me, or so I thought. As the presentation continued, it all became much clearer and more familiar.

Although *liminal space* is a term from the field of psychology, the host made a point to define it in layman's language: the space between what was and what is to come. The word *liminal* actually translates from the Latin word "limi," which means threshold. As we stand on a threshold, we are leaving one space but have not yet entered the new space. Think about the threshold on your front door. It is not really outside the house or inside, but in between.

This place, or space, was described as a type of limbo, often a place of extreme discomfort. For me, that was not the case. Liminal space, as I had experienced it, was a place of unbounded opportunity and potential. It was a place where we are unfettered by our past and yet fully alert to the possibilities and the potential ahead of us. In this space, we find our best chance to create the future.

I remember a visit to this "space" early in my career. Our team realized we did not have an adequate mechanism for listening to our customers. We knew we had to move past our antiquated methods, but we were unsure how to proceed. Some may have found this daunting and unsettling, maybe even uncomfortable—we had many years of experience and some degree of comfort with the old approach. I found this in-between state invigorating—what an opportunity. Just imagine what we could create!

As a result of that season in liminal space, today, many years later, our organization has received feedback from literally millions of customers. When you find yourself in between what was and what is to come, grab a flip chart or a whiteboard and dream.

As the conference unfolded, we were encouraged to be mindful when we find ourselves in liminal space to steward it well. Our guide suggested that in this liminal space, creativity and innovation flourish. I certainly didn't disagree with his conclusion, but I didn't like the implied reactionary posture: "When we *find* ourselves there." As if some lucky day, we might accidentally find ourselves on the threshold of breakthrough ideas and transformation. This didn't feel strategic enough to me.

Many leaders occasionally wander into liminal space and often good things do come of it. As I reflect on my early career, I was one of those leaders who haphazardly entered liminal space from time to time. Even as I considered my own experience, it was all too random. If liminal space is the domain of the new and unexpected, the place where innovation lives and the birthplace of new ideas, I want to go there often. But how?

What I've discovered since is the best leaders do go there often. They *choose* to stand on the threshold and look into the past while also turning their gaze to the future. This is no accident—it is a personal discipline. They create these threshold moments and consciously pause in this space to consider the possibilities, weigh the consequences of their actions, and chart their courses. This place is called *margin*.

YOU MUST MAKE TIME TO LEAD

For the purposes of this book, I have chosen a very focused definition of margin—the time and space needed to reflect, assess, think, create, and plan. Do you have time and space for these critical activities? Without them, you will forever be reacting, like a ship without an anchor or a rudder. If these disciplines are absent, you will be unable to lead well, escape the quicksand, and scale your impact. As if that is not enough incentive, Richard Rohr writes, "Without liminal space (margin) in our lives, we start idealizing normalcy." This is the last thing leaders need.

A leader's primary role is to *create* the future. Our vision for the future should never be an extension of the present or a return to the past. Normal is the realm of a manager who sees his or her role as controlling what is. The leader, by contrast, doesn't want to control—she seeks to release the potential of her people and her organization. There is nothing normal about a preferred future. Without the liminal space, escaping normalcy is unlikely, and so is a better tomorrow.

Michael Porter and Nitin Nohria invested many years studying CEOs. One of their findings: these leaders spent, on average, 28 percent of their working hours alone.[1] How are you doing on this front? I'm not suggesting a magical number. Who knows if 28 percent of your fifty, sixty, or seventy weekly working hours is correct? Only you know. But their finding could serve as a mirror. How are you doing, really? This is a crucial question. I would argue the most important hours of your week as a leader are those when you are alone. As Stephen Covey reminded us, "Private victories precede public victories."

When we create margin, we can gain a higher level of clarity than we can ever achieve in our day-to-day, nonstop activities. This clarity we so desperately need can be eclipsed entirely by our proximity to the problems and challenges we must ultimately respond to. Leaders can easily lose perspective if they are too close to the action for too long. This is an ever-present challenge, but it is not new.

In *The Secret*, Ken Blanchard and I referred to this as the heads-up, heads-down challenge. Heads-up work is always done best when you are above the daily fray. Ronald Heifetz, in his book *Leadership Without Easy Answers*, refers to this stepping away from the action as "going to the balcony." From there, he suggests, you can gain perspective.[2] Call it a balcony, a fire tower, or a stepladder, anything that allows you to pull up, to gain, or regain the proper view is essential.

Without conscious effort, the gravitational pull of today will keep us locked in a short-term, heads-down mode, blind to what could or should be the future. From time to time, we must pull up, deliberately putting some distance between ourselves and the activities of the day if we want to lead well. Only in the distance can we create the proper perspective.

Margin is not natural. As Aristotle posited, "Nature abhors a vacuum." Human beings are typically willing to serve as nature's agent and fill every minute of every day with activities. The absence of margin, however, leaves leaders struggling for insight, frustrated, and lacking credible plans to move forward. These conditions destine them and the organizations they serve to stay firmly mired in the grips of the quicksand they have chosen to inhabit.

OUR TIME MACHINE

Margin allows leaders to look both back in time and toward the horizon. From the threshold, the leader can see the past and the future. Margin becomes our time machine. In it, we find more than an opportunity to step out of the busyness. We position ourselves to gain and maintain perspective and clarity of mind, both essential if we wish to do our job well.

The first stop in our time machine is the past. This can be measured in days, weeks, months, or years, depending on what you are looking for. The principle in play is simple: The past is a veritable treasure trove of insight and wisdom, but like most treasure, we must search for it.

The words of European philosopher George Santayana are particularly applicable to leaders, "Those who do not remember their past are condemned to repeat their mistakes."[3]

You are unlikely to remember the details from your past, much less learn from it, without time for reflection and a focused assessment. Margin is the place for this historical perspective to emerge from the mist of time and faded memory. You will want to ask yourself challenging questions about your past efforts. Questions such as the following:

- What did I do to contribute to our success?
- What did I do, or fail to do, that contributed to our shortcomings?
- What actions or decisions would we repeat if given the chance?
- What would we do differently, given the same opportunity again?
- What other lessons should we remember as we create the future?

Let your imagination be your guide. In this part of your journey, you should wear several different hats—those of a historian, anthropologist, detective, and leader.

We certainly need to learn from the past, but we should never live there. As valuable as your look back will be, thankfully, your time machine can also beam you into the future.

Our primary role as a leader is to create positive change. How can we build what we cannot see? How can we see what we are not looking for? What is the future we want to build? What is the vision? These are not simple questions. On the contrary, they can be gut-wrenching, mind-boggling questions with virtually infinite possible responses. Margin is the place where we take what we've learned from the past and use it as input to think, create, and plan our tomorrow. We are the architects of the future, and margin is our drawing board.

HOW TO CREATE MARGIN IN YOUR WORLD

Admittedly, the world we live in wars against margin. The tsunami of information crashing over us on a daily basis and the rising tide of expectations both carry a false hope of progress born of our personal sacrifice. Nonetheless, I know many leaders who still prioritize margin and reap the benefits on a regular basis.

There are countless ways to create margin. In this section, I'll share a few proven practices, but you have to figure out what works for you—and what works can change due to life circumstances, job responsibilities, health factors, and more. What's most important is that you embrace the idea of creating margin like a dog with a bone—never letting it go; you can, and should, hold the tactics more loosely.

Before we jump into tactics, it's important to understand what margin is not.

- **Margin is not a vacation.** You need a vacation from time to time. However, rest and recreation are topics we'll cover in the chapter Expand Your Energy. The margin we're discussing here is a life and leadership tool.

- **Margin is not time to do email.** Yes, we are often drowning in email. Personal productivity matters, and there are entire books written on how to manage your email more effectively. Margin is so precious; please don't forfeit it for the sake of busy work.

- **Margin is not extracurricular.** Margin is not something you do only *if* you have time. Because our primary role as a leader is to create positive change, I don't know how you can do it well without margin. Margin should never be considered optional. I'll go a step further—the busier you are, the more responsibility you have, the more people you lead, the higher the stakes, the more you need margin. "I'm too busy for margin" is never the right answer.

So what can margin look like in the real world? Here are a few ideas to jump-start your thinking:

Focus Days

I am so fortunate to have worked with leaders who understand the power of margin. I know this may not be your experience, but perhaps you could be that leader for the next generation in your organization.

I remember, as a young leader, I was encouraged to invest one day a month at the library. Here's what I recall from the conversation.

Leader: I think you should schedule a day a month to go to the library.
Me: Why would I do that?
Leader: To think, to reflect, to plan.
Me: Umm . . . really?
Leader: Did things work out like you wanted over the last month?
Me: Not exactly.

Leader: Fine, do you know why? What can you learn from your experience? What will you do differently next month based on what you learned? Have your priorities changed? If so, what changes do you need to make to your plan and your calendar going forward?

This brief exchange started a career-long practice. Rather than library days, I call them focus days, and they are a regular fixture on my calendar. Could you schedule a day a month entirely dedicated to margin? If not, maybe a half day? How about a couple of hours? I believe it would quickly become the most valuable time on your leadership calendar.

Morning Ritual

For thousands of years, there have been leaders who have chosen to create margin in their lives *every* morning. Granted, this can take many forms—reading, walking, meditating, stillness, and possibly personal spiritual practices. Regardless of the activity, it can be a time to assess, reflect, think, create, and plan the day. It can also be a good time to fill your heart and mind with gratitude for a new day and the opportunities it holds.

Daily Review

Similar to a morning ritual, some leaders practice a daily review. The activities in their review vary widely but can include identifying highlights from the day, lessons learned, action items duly noted, and an assessment of personal performance. Some leaders review how well they lived out their personal core values during the day. You may choose to set this time aside before you leave the office (or close your laptop if working remotely), or you may prefer to set aside a few minutes at the very end of the day.

Regardless of when you do it, a daily review can be a valuable time of margin making.

Some leaders do both a morning and an evening session. Experiment with both and see where you derive more value. When I engage in this form of margin, it is primarily as described—a review. If that is how you approach this practice, it will still add value but will most likely not meet all your needs for margin.

Personal Retreats

This is a relatively new practice for me; I wish I had adopted it earlier in my career. My limited experience with these dedicated times away has been transformational. I know leaders who do these retreats regularly—some do them quarterly, some semiannually, and others annually. One of my mentors has built his annual calendar around his retreats and will often invest *days* reflecting, assessing, thinking, creating, and planning. He is one of the wisest human beings I've ever known. I wonder if there is a connection?

After Action Reviews

One of the highlights of working on this book was spending a few hours with a retired three-star general. During his distinguished career, he led many campaigns and served as the superintendent at West Point. Our interview team was reminded that margin is most often thought of as an individual discipline, and it usually is. However, we were challenged to embrace margin as a team discipline as well.

The perfect illustration of this is the widely held military practice called the After Action Review (AAR), designated time after every mission or exercise to debrief. "What went well? What didn't go well? Why not? What will we do differently in the future?" To embrace and inculcate this simple practice could introduce your entire organization to the value of margin as a collective discipline.

Add to this list, combine some of these practices, modify these ideas, discover what works for you, and build intentional margin into your schedule.

Although the list of specific tactics could go on for pages, I want to go back to the Smart Choice this section is built upon—the best leaders choose to Grow Capacity. You may be looking at the ideas above and thinking, "All of these ideas require time, and time is the one thing I don't have."

MARGIN IN THE MOMENT

Let's revisit the thoughts of Viktor Frankl:

> *Between stimulus and response there is a space. In that space is our power to choose our response. In our response lies our growth and our freedom.*

Frankl's insight is one for the ages. One of the many implications is what I have chosen to call *margin in the moment.* This single idea can elevate your leadership in profound ways.

When we began to see this idea of margin emerging in our research, a member of the team commented that many martial arts teach and train their students to enter the same space Frankl described. We were immediately captivated by the idea. Because I have a dear friend and mentor who happens to be a martial arts grand master, the team agreed a call was in order.

Jack, a student and teacher of kung fu for more than fifty years, confirmed our research findings. He said that kung fu is not a physical discipline but rather a mental one. He said he has been practicing and training students to enter the space Frankl described for decades. Jack also reminded us, when facing someone who intends to do you harm, the stakes can be very high. If you can't enter this space and choose the appropriate response quickly, the outcome could be painful.

So how do you create margin in the moment?

I've taken what we've learned and created a mental checklist for you to use to create margin in the moment. In cases where you have even more than a moment, these four steps may still provide a helpful guide.

1. **Stop.** Hit the pause button on our biases, history, emotions, and immediate reactions to the situation at hand. Simply stop. This is the learned ability to escape the moment—even if only for a moment. Clarity is hard to find when you're in motion.

2. **Listen.** You need to listen with your whole being. Listen with your ears, your brain, your intuition—look carefully, pay attention. What is actually happening? What are people really saying? What is true that is not being said?

3. **Think.** What are the options? What is possible? What's worked in the past? What if we tried something different? Is there an insight I'm missing? Are there clues to the way forward? What is the best possible outcome? How could I help make that outcome a reality? What would a more experienced and gifted leader do in this situation?

4. **Decide.** What is my best next step? What am I uniquely positioned to do in this situation? How can I add maximum value here? What actions could I take to have the greatest long-term benefit? What action has the highest probability of no regrets?

Just imagine the power you could harness if you could summon margin on demand. These four steps may represent the key you've been looking for, but the key will not insert itself into the lock. You and I must discipline ourselves to stop, listen, think, and decide *before* we respond.

I'm still a huge fan of more traditional forms of margin: planned, scheduled, and cherished time. But I believe margin in the moment is too valuable to ignore. I love the quote from Maria Edgeworth, "If we take care of the moments, the years will take care of themselves."

BE SMART!

At some point in the next thirty days, schedule one four-hour block of time for margin. (If this is too much of a stretch goal for you at this point, schedule a two-hour block.) Put it on your calendar now and protect it fiercely. Your assignment is simple: reflect, assess, think, create, and plan. Review the tips above for what to do and not to do during your time (no email!). You can thank me later.

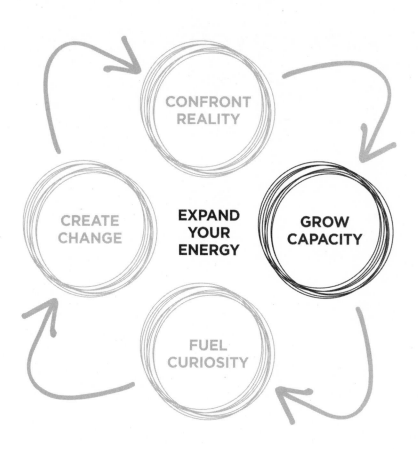

EXPAND YOUR ENERGY

"Energy and persistence conquer all things."
Benjamin Franklin

Some years ago, a friend of mine had an experience that changed his life forever. Don had just finished writing a successful memoir when his life stalled. During what should have been the height of his success, he found himself unwilling to get out of bed, avoiding responsibility, even questioning the meaning of life. One day while watching the Tour de France and pretending he was riding a bike, he had an epiphany. Pretending to ride a bike was a lousy story. So he bought a bike, joined a club, and ended up riding coast to coast. Now, that's a *much* better story!

Don Miller went on to write about this insight and others in his book *A Thousand Miles in a Million Years*. He learned the story we tell ourselves has a direct impact on our energy and motivation. We all want to live a better story. The power to write that story is largely in our hands.

Many of you have already written the story that, at least in your mind's eye, is crystal clear—a lot of you have already bought the bike, yet you still sit on the sofa of your life lacking the energy to hit the streets. That's why this chapter and all the strategies and tactics to follow matter. It's time to get on the bike and ride.

ENERGY FOR ALL THINGS

For many years, I thought my naturally high energy level would carry me indefinitely into the future. One of the problems with this overly optimistic worldview was my concept of energy. I thought of it exclusively in the physical realm. If I had enough energy to go to work, do things in the evening with my family, play an occasional round of golf, and do a few home projects along the way, I would be fine. Oh, and I forgot to mention, the more than occasional trip to the airport—I'm chasing two million miles in my frequent-flier status.

Maybe you assess your energy level in a similar fashion. I read an article years ago that proclaimed stamina as a leadership essential. Assuming you define stamina as having sufficient energy to do the things I mentioned above, I agree. If you cannot physically muster the energy to do the work, you essentially take yourself out of the game. Articles like the one I just described, although true in part, fueled my narrow and shallow thinking about energy.

My beliefs were fueled by youth, immaturity, and ignorance. The problem with my worldview on energy was simple: I was wrong. Energy is a much bigger topic than I understood at the time. Physical energy is essential, but it is just the beginning.

Another form of energy rarely discussed is mental energy. Yes, we require physical energy to get up and go to work, but what happens when we get there? Studies show millions of people experience brain fog during some portion of the day. Just to be clear, the fog I am describing is not a medical diagnosis, but rather a description of numerous symptoms affecting your ability to think. The signs include the inability to focus, trouble remembering things, disorganization, confusion, challenges articulating your thoughts, and more.[2]

Have you ever driven in fog? If so, think about what happens. For me, the first thing you do is slow down. This is not only prudent, but also a survival response. It's also hard to maintain perspective; you can easily become disoriented. The familiar is no longer recognizable. The signs along the roadside are obscured, the typical reference points are blotted out, and sometimes you can't even see the road itself. It's not fun to drive in a heavy fog; neither is it fun to lead in one.

What is the fog in our daily lives, and where does it come from? Although brain fog has many potential root causes, including medication, stress, chemical imbalances, pregnancy, depression, and other medical conditions, there are some causes we can address—sleep, diet, and exercise to name a few. More on these later. For now, let's agree: the role we play as leaders requires far more than showing up and going through the motions. We need mental energy.

As leaders, we can make the case that we are paid for our judgment and our decisions—the work of our minds, not the work of our hands. How can we fulfill our roles if we are running on fumes? Low mental energy is like a child's toy in need of new batteries. The actions are still there, but they become slower and slower as the battery is drained. We need both physical and mental energy to perform at our full potential. But wait—there's more.

What else could we need energy for beyond our minds and bodies? How about our relationships? All of us have relationships in our lives that give us energy and relationships that drain our energy. Although we have some control of this in our personal lives, in our working world, we have no choice. We have to work with all types of people regardless of how we connect with them at a personal level. This requires energy.

Some leaders who experience this workplace drain on their relational energy never name it. And since they haven't identified the important role that energy plays in their relationships, relationships continue to suffer. The most tragic part of this from my perspective is when those we love the most are often cheated the most. Here's how this can happen.

You have a demanding role as a leader in a growing organization; your team is expanding with your responsibilities. The work is challenging, and you love it. But to do all that is required of you drains all of your energy on a daily basis—before you return home to your family and friends. The tragedy is you don't have enough energy to maintain your critical personal relationships. The old line "I gave at the office" is painfully true. You and I need energy to fuel our minds, bodies, and relationships.

Anything else? Well, yes. In addition to physical, mental, and relational energy, the best leaders also have an ample supply of emotional energy. This is one of the arenas in which leaders can really strengthen or weaken their impact on those they lead, and unfortunately, it is often overlooked.

Here's how it works.

Your brain, working at a subconscious level, serves as the power station, allocating the energy you have each day until it is gone. The software that ultimately makes the energy-routing decisions functions based on a clear hierarchy of needs.

The first priority goes to the physical demands, and for many leaders, this requires all they have in store. But assuming you have more energy, the next allotment goes to the mental activities on your agenda—the decisions you need to make and the judgment calls that are at the heart of a leader's value to your organization. Let's move forward with the belief you have more to give. What's next? Your key relationships at work and in your personal life. Assuming you had a good day (not too taxing), much to your family's delight, you can engage with them in a meaningful way. So far, so good, at least for now.

Now we enter this final domain, emotional energy. At the end of the day, do you have anything left to give?

I just completed a couple of courses at the Stanford d.school on emergent interviewing. We were learning how to go beyond merely identifying *what* people did and go with them into the realm of *why* they did what they did. As we learned, for many people, this is unknown territory. Prompting someone to go deep inside their own life experiences and answer questions they have never previously considered is powerful.

One of the big reminders for me during the coursework was the power of empathy, to literally enter into the experience of another human being and feel what they are feeling. If someone is grieving, you go there too. If they are jubilant, you celebrate with them. This is something the best leaders do. For some, it may be a God-given talent, but for most of us, it is a skill that can be learned. But here is the kicker: empathy is a skill powered by energy. No energy, no empathy.

If you and I have used our stores of energy on the physical, mental, and relational demands of our work, we will not have the capacity to empathize. We need emotional energy, too, if we want to maximize our impact and contribution.

The bottom line is that leaders need an ever-ready store of energy. That's why the best leaders don't rely exclusively on their natural energy. They steward what they have and constantly choose to expand their stockpile at every opportunity. One of the worst feelings in the world is to see what needs to be done and not have the energy to engage. If this is a challenge you face, you can choose to live and lead differently.

CONDUCT AN ENERGY AUDIT

Here is a simple audit to recap where we've been in this chapter thus far and help you assess your current reality. As you think about your responses, use a five-point scale ranging from strongly disagree = 1 to strongly agree = 5. We've included a space for you to write in your answers. If you score a *five* on all four statements, you can skip to the next chapter. (Let me remind you there's absolutely no value in inflating your responses—you get to grade your own paper here, but those around you are grading your leadership every day.)

**Your
Score**

- I have an ample supply of physical energy to excel in life.
- I have enough mental energy to avoid the fog and think clearly, critically, and creatively throughout any given day.
- I have adequate energy to maintain productive and life-giving relationships at work and at home.
- I have sufficient energy available to fuel significant emotional connections.

OWN YOUR ENERGY

As we begin to go deeper on this topic, I have an uneasy feeling. I've been thinking about this issue for months and decided it would be best to name it here and now before we proceed. My concern has two components:

One, the typical leader will agree with the premise that we should find ways to manage, steward, and expand our energy. Yet most leaders consistently fail to make choices that replenish their energy.

I think this choice, perhaps more than any of the others you'll read about in this book, could be used as an example of what Jeffrey Pfeffer and Robert Sutton call the knowing-doing gap. One of their big ideas is that leaders can fall into the trap of collecting information (knowledge) without taking decisive action.[1] This concerns me as we move into an arena with an overabundance of common knowledge.

Second, I know from both my own experience and stories from countless leaders, the topic of energy, although generally viewed as important, is framed far too narrowly. As you read this chapter, I challenge you to think differently about energy and its impact on your leadership. Only then will you be able to successfully Grow Capacity.

Without some of the practices we are about to review, I'm fearful your leadership journey will likely be one of unfulfilled promise and unrealized potential. The content in this chapter matters far more than most leaders want to admit. Please read the following pages with an open heart and mind. I think your leadership potential may well hang in the balance.

We began with our overarching analogy of swimming in quicksand—could your fundamental problem be that you don't have enough energy to extricate yourself? Maybe you know what to do to alter your reality and just can't seem to get it done. It's not that you haven't tried. Most leaders understand the importance of energy. Yet, at the same time, it remains a huge issue.

In research for his book *The Secrets of CEOs*, Steve Tappin interviewed 150 global chief executives about business, leadership, and the harsh realities of their jobs. He told CNN, "Probably two-thirds of CEOs are struggling . . . The major emotions a CEO has are frustration, disappointment, irritation, and overwhelm." As part of his research, Steve's team also conducted physiological and neurological tests on chief execs. The results paint a picture of leaders overworked, overstressed, and exhausted.[3]

How do we turn the tide on this debilitating, career-limiting problem? You must have a plan. You have a plan for everything else, such as finances, expansion, innovation, business development, marketing, people, and more. Strategic planning is a big part of what leaders do. So why not create a plan for your own energy management?

YOUR ENERGY MANAGEMENT PLAN

We inspire, engage, and rally others to pursue our grand vision only if we have enough energy to do so. Those we serve are energized by the overflow and outpouring of our energy. You must increase your energy before you can lift others.

Our level of personal energy is both renewable and expandable—if we are intentional. Yet untold millions of leaders still struggle in this area. Without clear, specific, executable strategies and tactics for replenishment, you'll quickly overdraw your energy account. If you allow this to become a chronic deficit, you become bankrupt—sometimes referred to as burnout. Therefore, to avoid becoming a shell of a leader, forever mired in the quicksand of your life, you must choose to expand your personal energy supply. There are several key levers you can use to make this choice come to life.

Exercise

We're not going to dwell on this because you know this already. Physical exercise creates energy. A strong body has more energy than a weak one. Exercise creates energy. I know it may not feel like it in the moment, but it does. I don't really enjoy the exercise itself, but I love the benefits: physical, psychological, emotional, and increased energy levels. I am a better human being and a better leader when I exercise—you will be too.

If exercise is as hard for some of you as it is for me, I'll share one idea that may help—kedging. This is a practice I've used for decades. The word has nautical roots. It is the idea of taking an anchor away from a ship, dropping it, and then pulling the ship to the anchor. In terms of exercise, pick an event or activity you want to accomplish at some point in the future, such as "I am going to run a marathon in the spring of next year." Drop your anchor there and create a plan that will pull you toward the goal. This approach may provide additional motivation for you. I generally do this several times a year and not always regarding exercise (this book is a product of this technique). Try it.

Fuel and Fluids

Diet and hydration are probably the last things you want to think about. I ate like a twelve-year-old much of my life. For many years, my two primary food groups were pizza and chocolate chip cookies. As I aged, I began having some issues, one being afternoon fatigue. I couldn't figure it out until somebody asked me what I typically ate for lunch. I wasn't even sure why that was relevant. This was before I knew your energy level in the middle of the afternoon is usually a factor of two things: what you had for lunch and how much sleep you had the night before (we'll talk about sleep in a moment). I changed what I ate for lunch and haven't had afternoon fatigue issues for many years.

Hydration is a big deal too. Are you drinking enough water? A hydrated body is a healthier and more energetic body. I first came to appreciate how important water is on my first high-altitude trek. My guide, appropriately named Teacher, told me, "Water is medicine." I drank more than ever and reached the summit at just over 19,000 feet above sea level. When I returned home, to a much lower elevation, I found water is medicine here too. Consult your doctor regarding how much water you should drink. My guess is she will tell you to drink a lot more than you are today.

Think of your body like a Ferrari, Lamborghini, Maserati, pick your brand. If you owned one of these supercars, would you put sand in the gas tank? Of course not. You are responsible for something far more valuable than a supercar. You are the steward of your body. Think about your earning potential over your lifetime, not to mention all the good you can do for the world. If you put sand in the gas tank, you risk it all. What you eat and drink matters.

Sleep

If you were going to make a list of the most pressing issues leaders face around the world, I'm guessing many of you would include things like: lack of resources, corrupt governments, an unstable economy, inflation, deflation, warring neighbors, and more. And all of these would be legitimate responses. However, your list would be incomplete if you did not include the growing global threat of sleep deprivation.

Here are a few hard-to-believe statistics:

- A Gallup study found 40 percent of Americans are clinically sleep-deprived, while 70 percent admit they aren't getting enough sleep.[4]
- A UK study found that sleep-deprived people are seven times more likely to feel helplessness and five times more likely to feel lonely.[5]
- The National Highway Safety Administration links 1.2 million accidents and eight thousand deaths annually to "drowsy driving."[6]
- The wearable-device company, Jawbone, has now begun sharing global data; the sleep epidemic is now a pandemic. In Tokyo, residents sleep only five hours and forty-five minutes per night. Seoul—six hours and three minutes, and Dubai— six hours and thirteen minutes.[7]
- The sleep crisis in the United States, Japan, UK, Germany, and Canada is estimated to cost a staggering $680 billion per year.[8]
- Lack of sleep has been linked to *seven of the top fifteen* leading causes of death in the United States—our lack of sleep is literally killing us.[8]

What does this have to do with leadership? Leaders may be the most vulnerable group of all. Our wiring, temperament, and breadth of responsibilities immediately puts us in the high-risk category.

When we don't get enough sleep, it affects our energy and our mental acuity the same way increasing our blood alcohol level does. Without sufficient sleep, leaders make a lot of decisions as if they're under the influence of alcohol. You constantly see campaigns against drunk driving; we probably need some against leading while drunk (from lack of sleep).

This topic reminds me, once again, my mother was right. She started telling me I needed more sleep when I was a teenager. Today, my energy is as good as it has ever been, in part because I am heeding Mom's advice and getting more sleep.

My mom was not alone in her advocacy for sleep. In her best-selling book *The Sleep Revolution*, self-proclaimed sleep evangelist Arianna Huffington[9] shares some fascinating stories from the world of professional sports; both individual players and teams seem to be waking up to the promise of sleep. Here's one of my favorites.

Andre Iguodala of the Golden State Warriors decided to change his sleep habits. The results: his three-point shot percentage doubled, his free-throw percentage increased by 8.9 percent, and his turnovers decreased by 37 percent.[9]

If sleep drives performance on the hardwood and in the boardroom, how much sleep is enough? Only you, your body, and your physician can set the exact amount of sleep you need. However, the data from the Centers for Disease Control and Prevention suggests the amount of time required to support good health (and energy) changes throughout your life. For adults, they recommend seven-plus hours per night.[10] The Mayo Clinic suggests some adults may need up to nine hours a night to thrive.[11] Keep in mind that other factors impact your actual sleep quality. If sleep is an issue for you, commit to learn more and make this part of your energy management plan.

Recreation

I don't know if you have any recreation in your life or not, but you should. It is a vital source of energy. Decades ago, a leader told me I worked too much. He suggested some planned recreation. His challenge was for me to think about the word itself differently.

We tend to think of recreation as fun, frivolity, and idleness. He suggested I look at the word *recreation* more carefully. It's re-*creation*. If you want to have maximum impact in the world, you need the discipline of recreation. It will give you energy.

When it comes to recreation, I'm not sure what you do matters as much as the fact that you do something. The only criteria I can come up with is that you find an activity that replenishes you. I have friends who golf, read, garden, run (I still don't see how this can be recreational), hike, watch old movies, and more. What fills you up and is not work related? Do more of that and you should find yourself with more energy to invest in all areas of your life and leadership.

Relationships

My hope and prayer is every one of you has some life-giving relationships. If not, I would encourage you to make this a priority. If you have never experienced the joy of hanging out with people who breathe life into you, I think you'll quickly find it intoxicating. These could be your best friends or simply individuals who you find interesting and inspiring. Try making a list of three or four people who already meet these criteria in your life or begin the process of identifying others who might.

While we are talking about relationships, do you have any ongoing relationships that suck the life out of you? If so, you may need to fire some friends, or at least find ways to limit your time with these people. You need energy to live and lead at your full potential—you don't need any toxic relationships working against you. The concept of unfriending somebody is bigger than Facebook. It might actually help you as you try to muster enough energy to do all the things you want to do in your life and leadership.

Purpose

In his poem "Walden," Ralph Waldo Emerson wrote, "In each pause we heard the call." For most people, the call, or their sense of personal purpose, is energizing. Is your purpose clear? If you are trying to maintain your energy for the long haul, I suggest you affirm your purpose. This is not intended to be a mysterious process, although I am surprised by the number of people I meet who have no idea why they exist.

If you don't have clarity on this all-important question, I believe your leadership will suffer. Not only will you miss the energy generated by clarity, perseverance in the face of difficulty may be challenging. The call transcends the work of the day. Your purpose is why you believe you were born. Your purpose is what gives ultimate meaning to your labor. Your purpose should give you the courage to do the hard work of leadership.

One word of encouragement here: if you don't have clarity on your purpose, it is never too late. We talked earlier about the power of margin in a leader's life. We said it was a time to reflect, assess, think, create, and plan. If you have work to do on clarifying your purpose, margin is the perfect place to wrestle with this issue. Also, once you have something, hold it loosely—you should always reserve the right to get smarter. What is clear to you today may be even clearer tomorrow.

Spiritual Practices

Where do you really derive your strength? Many successful people attribute their effectiveness to the grounding they receive from personal spiritual disciplines. These can include a wide array of activities: solitude, journaling, prayer, silence, meditation, service, reading ancient texts, gratitude, worship, and more. When attempting to increase your energy, don't overlook forces beyond your control and comprehension.

––––

We must have enough energy for ourselves and to share with others. The people we serve look to us for inspiration. They look to us for empathy. They look to us to lead well. These expectations require a tremendous amount of energy. I'm thankful we have multiple wells we can draw from to fill our tanks.

BE SMART!

Pick one of the energy-boosting strategies from this chapter (hydration, sleep, relationships, recreation, etc.) and make a commitment to yourself to incorporate the practice into your daily routine for *thirty days*. At the end of the month, I would love to hear what you discovered. If you are willing to share your story, you can email me at Mark@SmartLeadershipBook.com. I promise not to share your identity—I just want to cheer you on.

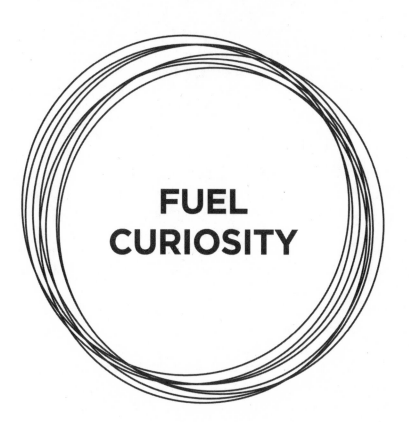

FUEL
CURIOSITY

FUEL CURIOSITY

"I have no special talents. I am only passionately curious."
Albert Einstein

n 2003, I met a man named Fergal Quinn. At the time he was the CEO of a grocery chain in Ireland called Superquinn. As I recall, he had about thirty stores. He was also the Irish equivalent of the US Postmaster General for their country and a member of the Irish Parliament. He was a very talented, high-capacity leader. We had the privilege to visit Fergal in Ireland before we invited him to speak to our entire organization. Of his many noteworthy traits, none surpassed his insatiable curiosity.

One of the clues which revealed Fergal's unquenchable desire to learn was the amount of time he invested talking to his customers—his commitment was akin to an obsession. Let's be clear: I have known many CEOs who cared deeply about their customers, but Fergal was on a different level.

The practice that differentiated him from any CEO I have ever met and demonstrated his curiosity most vividly was the fact that, every week, he personally conducted a focus group with his customers. I feel like I need to say that again: *every single week*, Fergal conducted a focus group with customers.

When was the last time you talked to your customers? Or the better question might be: When was the last time you *listened* to customers? What fueled Fergal's passion for his weekly meetings? His love for his customers and his boundless curiosity.

I believe curiosity is underrated and undervalued by our world. Yet the best leaders seem to have found a way to leverage this innate power. As a result, their curiosity is often the unsung hero behind their creativity, adaptability, innovation, and impact.

WE WERE BORN THIS WAY

Some leaders may assume they didn't receive their allotment of curiosity at birth, or, through no fault of their own, they were the recipient of a "curiosity-ectomy." Neither of these beliefs is true. However, as a result of these misplaced beliefs, these leaders far too often rely on copycat or late-to-market solutions in an attempt to do what others have already done. Rarely do leaders who fail to flex their curiosity muscles innovate or lead others to do so. It is essential for every leader who desires maximum impact and longevity to learn how to Fuel Curiosity.

Leaders do not need a curiosity transplant; it is already in us. It may be dormant, latent, or hiding—buried deep within the recesses of our spirit—but it is there. Think for a moment about how infants learn—they try things. And as soon as they can begin to speak, they ask questions. Unfortunately, the world has a systemic bias against curiosity and the creativity that often resides in its wake.

Consider an example cited by Roger von Oech in his classic book *A Whack on the Side of the Head*. When Roger was a sophomore in high school, his teacher drew a dot on the chalkboard and asked the students what she had drawn. After a prolonged silence, finally, one brave young man said, "It's a dot on the chalkboard." Everyone appeared to be relieved that someone had courageously given the correct answer. That was all they could muster. The teacher said,

"I'm surprised. I did the same exercise with a group of kindergarten students yesterday and they came up with fifty different things it could be: an owl's eye, a cigar butt, the top of a telephone pole, a squashed bug, and more."[1]

You might wonder what happened between age five and age fifteen, and twenty-five, and forty-five? A lot! The onslaught of curiosity-killing moments may have actually begun in kindergarten when a child drew a purple apple and a well-meaning teacher said, "Apples are not purple; they are red." Even this response fails to acknowledge the green and yellow ones!

And thus, the world of "one right answer" was unveiled to children at a very early age and reinforced year after year. Because there was already a right answer, there was no reason to explore, to pursue alternatives, or to create an alternate hypothesis. Your job, as you came to believe, first as a child, and later an adult, was to conform and learn the predetermined answers to the questions. This is not generally a world conducive to questions like "Why?" or "Why not?"

There's much more that could be said about the systematic, almost universal, conspiracy against curiosity and the consequences it has on organizations. However, I think a more productive conversation is how and why the best leaders have chosen to do just the opposite—rather than suppress curiosity, they intentionally fuel it; you can too.

THE SMART CHOICE

Choose to Fuel Curiosity to maintain relevance and vitality in a changing world.

How stable is your world? I know that's a big question so let me focus it for you.

- How have your customers' expectations changed over the last twelve months?
- How have your employees' expectations changed since you first became a leader?
- How have your organization's strategies changed in the last five years?
- How have your personal goals and aspirations shifted as you've progressed in your career?
- How has technology impacted your business?
- How has foreign competition made your work more challenging?

The late Stephen Covey, author of *The 7 Habits of Highly Effective People*, talked about a world of perpetual white water. Have you ever been white water rafting or kayaking? In the white water, you are flooded by not only water but also adrenaline. Your mind and body are called upon to make split-second decisions during periods of hyperfocus. I'm not sure this describes everyone's world, but few successful leaders today are on a float trip down a lazy river with a drink in one hand and a book in the other.

I'm guessing the water in your world is probably getting choppy; if it hasn't already, I predict it will soon. That's one of the reasons the world needs you to be more curious and creative than ever before. Not just well-versed on what worked yesterday or last year, we need leaders who have the willingness to explore the possibilities presented by the future. We need leaders to help people navigate the white water. How do we do this?

- We must see a vision beyond the waves.
- We push for solutions others deem impossible.
- We ask different questions.
- We are willing to learn from others.
- We care about today, but we work to ensure there will be a better tomorrow.

Where do all of these activities find their energy? Curiosity.

So if you are a believer in the power of curiosity, the biggest challenge is how to bring yours back to the forefront of your day-to-day leadership. How do you Fuel Curiosity? It begins with the Smart Choice to do so.

THE CASE FOR CURIOSITY

Let's take a quick look at what's at stake if we fail to Fuel Curiosity.

In his book *Barbarians to Bureaucrats*, Larry Miller took Arnold Toynbee's study of twenty-one extinct civilizations and mapped their behaviors with modern corporate life cycles—the patterns were the same. One of the most intriguing insights for me was a key signal of demise, in both civilizations and organizations:

> *When leaders begin to apply yesterday's solutions to today's problems, the end is inevitable.*[2]

This has always been a sobering reminder to me as a leader. Am I guilty of trying to make yesterday's answers fit today's challenges? More importantly, how do we avoid the trap of success? This terminal tendency to over-rely on yesterday's answers always presents itself at the zenith of the civilization and the organization. Is demise our destiny? What can leaders do to extend the life, relevance, and vitality of the organizations they lead? Curiosity is the antidote. But it is one we must choose in the face of challenge.

Curiosity is rarely welcomed, particularly in a season of success. "If it's not broken, don't fix it" is a popular refrain from many short-sighted, "successful" leaders. Examples of this are too numerous to count. A few of the better known are Kodak, who invented the digital camera but squandered the opportunity for fear it would cannibalize their film business. Or Blockbuster, who failed to see the formidable challenge posed by Netflix, rebuffing their offer to be acquired. Or the entire music industry, who said, "Sue Napster." Today, more than two decades after the record industry did "sue Napster," their sales are about half (in inflation-adjusted dollars) compared to the day Napster launched.[3]

The leaders who do choose to Fuel Curiosity bring a life-giving gift to those they lead. It is a gift that gives and gives and gives.

Curiosity Pays Dividends in the Short and Long Term

An inquisitive spirit can help you solve today's problems, but equally important, it helps you envision a rich and prosperous future. Some of the gems you'll pick up along the way will have immediate value and application; others will increase in value over time or when a unique opportunity presents itself years down the road.

For example, I have built relationships with leaders around the world through my travel and speaking. There are certainly short-term benefits from these connections—camaraderie, sharing best practices, and in some cases, real friendships have developed. Recently, I needed help with a global culture study. I was able to call a leader on another continent to gain his perspective on our project. I met this leader over a decade ago, and I'm still enjoying the dividends today.

Curiosity Opens New Possibilities

The two simple words, "What if . . . ?" could become the key to the future of your organization. Far too many leaders can become ensnared by what is. When this happens, they forfeit what might be possible. The pursuit of new ideas is always on the agenda of the best leaders. They fully embrace their role as architects of the future. A curious mind is the birthplace of the future.

Curiosity Fuels Growth

The curious leader and organization have a bias for growth— personally, professionally, and for the entire organization. Learning is improving. Learning is living. Learning is essential to growth.

Without growth, there is only decline. No individual or organization can hang in suspended animation. Grow or decline—every leader must decide.

Curiosity Can Help Future-Proof Your Business

We don't know what the future holds, but leaders who fuel curiosity regularly venture into the future. Their spirit of exploration is energized by their curiosity. The future does not necessarily favor the prepared—it will favor the adaptable. Many organizations have been prepared for the wrong scenarios. Curiosity at the organizational level is a real competitive advantage.

Curiosity Sparks Creativity and Innovation

Creative thinking, simply defined, is the ability to generate alternatives. Without curiosity, the set of alternatives will be significantly reduced. "What happens if … ?" is a question born in a curious spirit. This question, and others like it, can provide the catalyst for new ideas and practices that translate into real value.

Curiosity Challenges Complacency

Many leaders and the organizations they lead are in a rut. This state of mind and the behaviors it spawns can easily become a deep hole of mediocrity. The desire to learn is a powerful antidote for the death rattle of complacency.

Curiosity Creates Energy

Of all the intangibles associated with curiosity, energy is often overlooked. I even hesitate to call it an intangible because I believe you can feel the difference in a learning organization fueled by individual and corporate curiosity and a static, close-minded workplace.

Curiosity Challenges Inertia

An object at rest remains at rest until acted upon by an outside force—I talked about this as one of the reasons some leaders are not willing to Confront Reality. When individuals within an organization are putting their curiosity to work, movement is created. The new ideas are the force needed to break free from the gravitational pull of the ordinary.

Curiosity Is Contagious

Have you ever had someone tell you about a new experience or hobby they have recently undertaken? How about a book they read or a place they visited? Do you remember how learning about their discovery piqued your own interest? Maybe not to take up the violin or travel to Paris, but when you share in another's joy of discovery, something stirs within you—you often want the same feeling their discovery generated.

Curiosity Will Improve Your Organization

In addition to all the benefits listed above, research conducted by Francesca Gino from Harvard confirms the following: curiosity triggers more creative decisions, increases the respect people have for their leaders, and inspires people to develop more collaborative relationships within the organization.[4]

When a leader chooses to Fuel Curiosity, starting with their own, and expects others to do the same, problems once thought unsolvable become the next success story. Curiosity is not only the key to unlock many of your most stubborn problems, it will also create a competitive advantage for tomorrow.

If I have done my job well, you look at the list above and say, "I need to invest more time and energy cultivating curiosity." What's holding you back? This is when I once again need to play my "I'm no psychologist" card. However, I do think in addition to the life-long deterrents I have already mentioned, there is a pragmatic, present-day reason many leaders take the path requiring the least amount of curiosity—capacity.

If you and I cannot generate sufficient capacity, we will never be able to rediscover the full depth and potential of our most curious, most creative selves. I mention this here, before we begin to explore strategies and tactics around curiosity, because I want to encourage you again—the four Smart Choices *all* matter and work *together.* When you make the Smart Choice to Grow Capacity, one of the by-products is you will have the capacity to Fuel Curiosity. Without capacity, a choice to Fuel Curiosity is like a bad check—one you can write but cannot cash.

REDISCOVER YOUR CURIOSITY

I promise the desire to learn and grow is still inside you. And as you learn to rediscover the curiosity of your youth, you will begin to escape the quicksand of today's world. In this chapter we will look at several suggestions to help you Fuel Curiosity. Then, we'll do a deeper dive into some of these ideas in the next few chapters.

Ask More and Better Questions

I remember a long time ago our organization made an investment in me and a large number of my colleagues by offering a workshop, the lessons from which still create value today. How many training sessions have you attended that you believe are still paying dividends decades later?

We were introduced to a guy named John Sawatsky. His specialty and the focus of our workshop: how to ask better questions. Something John said that day has stuck with me and probably will until I die: "If you ask better questions, you get better answers." As it relates to curiosity, I will add, "The *more* questions you ask, the more likely you are to learn something." I have a lot more to say about this topic in the next chapter.

Get Out More

There are many ways to do this, but one particularly productive method is to just talk to people. This may sound odd, but who you talk to matters. What would happen if you intentionally sought out interesting, diverse, and talented people to spend time with?

This strategy for fueling curiosity is enriching at many levels. Not only can you meet some amazing people, but you will also have the chance to experience what my Cajun friends call *lagniappe*, an unexpected gift.

When is the last time you had a meeting, or a meal, with someone "different"? If we're not intentional, it will likely be a long time between these opportunities. If you think this is a strategy you may want to employ, I suggest you have several hardworking, open-ended questions in mind before you arrive. Hold them loosely—you get no extra credit for asking all your questions. We will explore this idea in the upcoming chapter Talk with Strangers.

Test and Learn

Over the years, I have become fascinated with design thinking. For those who may not be familiar with the concept, it is an idea born in the d.school at Stanford University. Design thinking places the user at the center of the process. What does the user need? What does the user want? What problem is the user trying to solve? To answer these questions, and others like them, proponents of design thinking use a number of tools and techniques. One of their tried-and-true methods is the concept of test and learn. This practice, and mindset, could be a valuable way for you to accelerate your personal and organizational learning. At the same time, it could provide energy and vitality for your ongoing journey of discovery.

One form of this is often referred to as rapid prototyping. In your context, what is something you would like to learn or develop but lack the cash or the personnel to "do right"? Have you considered a low-cost, low-resolution experiment? Try it and see what you can learn. Then, try it again. Rapid prototyping creates test and learn opportunities—these always spark new questions and, often, new insights. Don't wait until everything is perfect to try something. Curiosity is often abandoned on the path to perfection.

Read

You may have heard the revelations regarding how many books a typical CEO reads in a year. Although the numbers vary widely, an internet search will reveal numbers between sixty and one hundred per year. For me, even in the absence of hard data, I believe top leaders are readers. As I reflect on this, several questions and conclusions come to mind.

One, CEOs are busy women and men. If they can find time to read, why is this such a struggle for me? Two, if a CEO with all the demands he or she has on their time, makes time for this, there must be value in the practice. Three, there may be more to this idea of reading than I previously thought.

Reading is generally accepted as the most efficient way to receive information. When we listen to someone speak, they typically do so at 100–130 words per minute. Our brains are capable of much faster processing rates (approximately eight hundred words per minute). According to Jim Kwik, human potential expert and author of *Limitless*, the average reader can consume two hundred words per minute. Armed with a few tips and some practice, you and I can easily improve this number to four hundred words per minute.[5] Therefore, my conclusion: the efficiency of reading is likely the primary reason so many CEOs invest the time.

While reading is the most efficient way to receive information, don't miss the real value: it is not the number of books completed, but the information those books contain. The knowledge acquired through an aggressive reading plan could be a primary fuel source for your curiosity and your success. That's also why it is important to read widely. To read one hundred leadership books certainly has value, but to read a few in adjacent disciplines or totally outside your interest can provoke ideas, questions, and insights to keep the fires of curiosity burning hot.

CAPTURE THE MAGIC AND THE MUNDANE

One of the consequences you will likely experience as you fuel your curiosity is a flood of new ideas and potential insights. What do you do with it all? How do you keep from losing these flashes of inspiration? Many curious minds over the ages have had a common practice of capturing their thoughts, quotes, questions, sketches, doodles, and more in personalized notebooks.

These books go by several names including the commonplace book (everything in a common place), the *zibaldone*, which in fifteenth-century Italy translated to "hodgepodge book," and the pillow book from fifteenth-century Japan compiled by Sei Shonagon. These books are not journals or personal diaries; they are more like personal scrapbooks. The only criteria for inclusion is the owner's personal interest in an entry.

There are examples from across the world and through the centuries of this practice. In the second century, Seneca and Marcus Aurelius kept books that fit this category. Leonardo da Vinci's notebooks fit the definition of a commonplace book. He described his notebooks like this: "a collection without order, drawn from many papers, which I have copied here, hoping to arrange them later each in its place, according to the subjects of which they treat."

These books gained huge popularity in the seventeenth century and the practice of compiling them was even taught in some universities, including Oxford and Harvard, as an essential skill.

John Locke, Francis Bacon, John Milton, Ralph Waldo Emerson, and Henry David Thoreau were all notable fans of this approach for capturing life's insights, questions, and curiosities.

I don't expect you to take this idea at face value or embrace it because a bunch of famous dead people did it. However, there are a few reasons I think you may want to experiment with creating your own commonplace book.

Capture Those Things That Capture Your Attention

We have so much going on in our world today. We are bombarded on every side by more information than is humanly possible to process. So it is easy to understand how we can forget things we wish we had not forgotten. I have developed a knack for remembering I have forgotten something. Although I work to avoid it, it happens more than I would like. Has this ever happened to you? My fear, and the data suggests, this collective and growing forgetfulness is not a figment of our imaginations. Our short-term memories are being eroded by the way we receive and process information.

If you have an idea or hear a quote, a book recommendation, or some concept that intrigues you, write it down. Even if you don't know what you will do with it, you are better to have it than not. Fragments are welcomed, and incomplete and ill-formed thoughts should be the norm. Your commonplace book is not a place for finished ideas; it is the jar in your cabinet full of random screws, nails, and rubber bands. Someday, you may find exactly what you are looking for in that jar.

Not only can you record your ideas, insights, and random thoughts in your commonplace book, but you can also document your struggles and stumbles. Failure can be a powerful teacher if we are paying attention. It's always good to ask: What did I learn today? Sometimes the answer will be associated with a mistake or missed opportunity. You may want to write these down with a "Note to Self:" Don't do that again!

Prevent Good Ideas from Evaporating

Have you ever laid down at night and, just before you drift off to sleep, an idea pops into your head? Tempted to get up and write it down or type it in your phone, do you ever say to yourself, "I'll remember this idea and write it down in the morning?" I have. Guess what—I usually forget. To make matters worse, I usually *remember* that I *had* an idea. I just have no idea what it was.

What's going on in this situation? Here's a quick explanation of another fascinating feature of our brain—as our brains begin to idle down (and crank back up after we've been sleeping), we go through a phase in which more theta waves are produced. While we are in this zone, we are more idea-prone.

Several creative geniuses of the last century discovered this phenomenon and harnessed it to their advantages. One notable story is about Thomas Edison. He would sit in a large stuffed chair or lie on a cot while holding lead weights. On the floor directly beneath the weights, he would place metal plates. Just as he would begin to doze off, he would drop the weights, which hit the pans to wake him. He would then go immediately back to his work. He knew from experience and experimentation that in these moments, he would often have his best ideas.

Little was said, or written, about this quirky habit of Edison during his lifetime. He didn't discuss it because he believed it gave him competitive advantage. Today, in the Edison & Ford Winter Estate garden in Ft. Myers, Florida, visitors can see a life-size bronze statue of Edison holding an iron ball about the size of a softball by his side.

Now, I'm not suggesting you sleep in a chair with weights and pie pans; what I am suggesting is that you should *always* capture your ideas *in the moment.* Specifically, if you are entering or emerging from a brain-induced moment of clarity. Your ideas and insights can be like lightning—brilliant for an instant and then gone. A commonplace book is a perfect tool to keep by your bedside and as an ever-present companion.

I realize we are living in the twenty-first century and the idea of a physical notebook may seem antiquated. Most of what I just described can be accomplished digitally. There is a catch—you may want to invest in hardware and software that allows you to use a stylus. There are numerous studies to support the advantages of handwritten notes over those captured with a keyboard.[6]

The process of writing vs. typing engages deeper levels of cognition. One other advantage of handwritten notes: there is less temptation to merely capture what you've just heard. Due to the slower rate of capture possible when taking handwritten notes, our tendency is to paraphrase or translate the idea as we write it down. This act alone intensifies the experience and aids in learning concepts.

Facilitate Review

If you don't have any notes to review, you cannot review them. I know you can theoretically review the mental notes you took during a meeting or while attending a conference. Good luck with that. My memory is not a fraction of what it was a few decades ago. I need a backup plan.

My dad was a notetaker. He kept his notes in his front shirt pocket. In the evening, he would pull them out and review them. I remember watching this daily ritual as a child. One day, I asked him about what he was doing. He said, "These are my paper brains. I have written down the things I said I would do for people today. If I didn't write them down, I might forget."

For my dad, his "paper brains" were a safety net. As you and I go through life, our commonplace book (physical or digital) can be our safety net to allow us to review not only the action items from the day but any other insights, ideas, quotes, quips, and questions that might serve us in the future. The review process alone will fuel our curiosity.

The important part here is to *review* your notes. My notes are organized predominantly by month, although I do have a few other digital notebooks for projects. I review the monthly notes at least a couple of times per month. The project notes tend to be accessed as needed. I cannot begin to count the number of times a review has sparked something else. That is how curiosity works.

It is no accident I chose the language Fuel Curiosity to represent this Smart Choice. Just as you can fuel a fire, my challenge is not merely to keep curiosity burning but to turn it into a raging inferno. Frequent review of my notes helps.

Personalize Your Collection to Meet Your Needs

One final reason I think commonplace books work for so many people is the personal nature of the approach. If you want a fun moment of inspiration, google images of commonplace books—you will see a world of variety. There is not one template or form to follow. You can be artistic or not; you can be linear in your notetaking or not. You can mix and match categories or have no categories at all.

Commonplace books are not intended to be seen by others. There should be no fear of judgment—no spell-check required. These are private notes on things you find noteworthy. Some of the ideas will be your own while others will be the thoughts of people you encounter. There is no requirement regarding how often you will make an entry, there's no minimum word count, and there is no pressure to have a compelling image to accompany your idea.

You may also find it helpful to develop your own shorthand and symbols to aid in review. I'll fight the urge to share mine because this is totally your decision. However, you may find it helpful to create a denotation for action items, questions for further thought and reflection, quotes, big ideas, and any other categories you choose, or not. If you do decide to create a commonplace book, make it your own.

ONE CHOICE TO RULE THEM ALL?

Is there one Smart Choice to rule them all? Probably not. Each brings its own unique power to our leadership. The choice to Fuel Curiosity, to learn and grow, is transformational—it is our fountain of youth. Our capacity to grow determines our capacity to lead.

One of my mentors was Howard Hendricks. He served as a professor at Dallas Theological Seminary (DTS) for over sixty years. He shared with me a story he said changed his life forever.

Hendricks was a student at DTS and had the unenviable task for a college student of working the breakfast shift in the cafeteria. Each morning, long before sunrise, as he made his way to the kitchen, he would pass the home of one of his professors. The young Hendricks could see through the window the man seated at his desk, apparently studying. Then, on many days, late in the evening, as Howard would retrace his path back to his dorm, he would see the professor still seated at his desk.

One day, Hendricks mustered the courage to ask the professor about his observation. "I see you at your desk early in the morning and still seated there late at night. How long have you been teaching here?"

"About twenty years," the professor said.

Hendricks responded, "Don't you have it figured out by now?" I think what Howard was really asking was "Can't you just use the same lecture notes year after year?"

The professor's response still echoed in Hendricks's heart and mind some sixty years later.

"I made a decision years ago I would rather have my students drink from a running stream than a stagnant pool."

This simple story had a profound impact on Hendricks, me, and hopefully, you. As leaders, I think we should all make that same pledge. The third Smart Choice to Fuel Curiosity will ensure we can always provide the cool, refreshing drink those we lead so badly need.

BE SMART!

Let's revisit the concept of test and learn. Think of something you would like to improve in your life or leadership. What type of low-resolution, low-cost test or prototype could you create? Build it. Try it. See what you learn and then try it again.

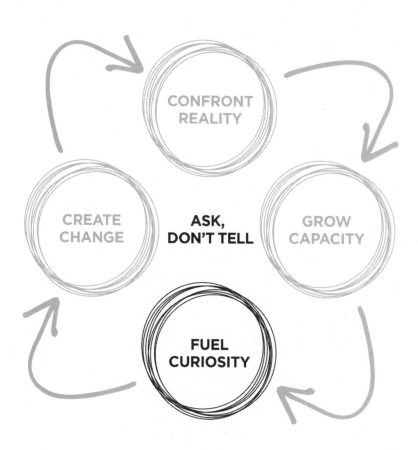

ASK, DON'T TELL

"The important thing is to not stop questioning."
Albert Einstein

Jim Collins is a global thought leader in the field of leadership. *Built to Last* and *Good to Great* are two of his books that have had profound impacts on millions of leaders. To know Jim personally and to have him speak at our annual event on two occasions has been a privilege. He has challenged and inspired me and all our leaders.

One of my favorite moments came when Jim began to talk about questions. He asked all of us to consider our question-to-statement ratio. He encouraged us to not only be aware of our current ratio—how often we ask a question versus making a statement—but he also suggested we double the number of questions. While I and the thousands assembled were still pondering the implications of a shift of that magnitude, he added, "And then double it again."

In a side conversation, Jim began to tell me about his sleep patterns. I was interested but wasn't quite sure why he was sharing this information. He then revealed that he was also tracking his questions, and apparently grading them based on their value. Jim had committed to getting more sleep, because when he did, he said he asked more good questions. Jim is no doubt a fan of questions.

How important are questions to you? How central are they to the way you lead? For me, the more questions I ask, the better I lead.

WHY QUESTIONS MATTER

Questions to a leader are like a pickaxe to a frontier miner. They can serve as your primary tool to unearth the nuggets of truth and insight you seek. Following are some of the reasons you should make questions an essential tool as you attempt to Fuel Curiosity and scale your impact.

Questions Make You Smarter

Whether we want to admit it or not, we don't know everything. When you ask a question, you have the opportunity to get smarter faster. If you ask someone about a project, an idea, a conference, a book, or a relationship, the answer they provide shortens the amount of time required for you to acquire the same information through personal experience. A software analogy may be helpful. When you ask a question and actually listen to the response, you are essentially adding a new line of code to your own programming.

Questions Make *Others* Smarter

When we ask a question, the recipient of our query will have to think. Even if their answer is, "I don't know," this revelation itself is knowledge. What if your follow-up question helps them understand a way forward or a next step? "How could you find the answer?" Or, "Who could help you find the answer?" Or, "Why do you think it might be important for you to know the answer?" These questions and countless others will help the people around you grow.

Questions Reveal Additional Information

Regardless of how much knowledge, information, and experience you have with a topic or subject, a few well-placed and thoughtful questions will reveal more information. I mentioned in an earlier chapter about the leadership development group I've been in for more than twenty years. We use a question-based study method. As a result, I continue to discover there is so much I do not know about this mysterious thing we call leadership. The answers have not been nearly as helpful as the questions for opening new paths of discovery.

Questions Can Transport You to a Place You've Never Been

There are many questions that can take you to another time and place (e.g., How do you think people will solve this problem in a hundred years? How do you think people would have solved this a hundred years ago?). Others are even more bizarre and thought-provoking. This is fantastic. Questions of this nature can jolt your imagination and shake you free of the shackles of today. Einstein said, "Problems cannot be solved on the same level of thinking at which they were created." These transport questions can really set your mind free. Even more pedestrian versions surrounding budgets, timing, and people in modern times can create an entirely new frame of mind and put you in a scenario you have probably never considered. Find more examples of these on the following pages.

Questions Spawn More Questions

A good question responded to thoughtfully almost always opens the door to another question. The ethnographic interviewing course I referenced earlier drilled this into my head. While listening to a response, we are actually listening at several levels: content, emotional charge, tone, word choice, and more. One of the most helpful things we should be listening for is an open door to ask another question. The insight you are seeking is often not behind the first, second, or third door but many layers deep into the conversation. The key to each door is another question.

Questions Demonstrate Your Openness and Humility

The prideful leader doesn't ask a lot of questions. When your team sees you willing to ask authentic questions, your stock will increase. Asking questions is not a sign of weakness—it is a sign of wisdom. People always watch the leader; when they see your willingness to be vulnerable and ask honest, thoughtful questions, they will do the same. This inquisitiveness will strengthen your leadership, your team, and your organization.

Questions Can Spark Creativity

The mind is a self-optimizing memory system with its hardwired tendency to follow known patterns and routines. Questions are one of the easiest ways to redirect your thinking. The questions don't even need to be particularly clever or thought-provoking. Simple questions such as "What else could we do?" Or, "What if . . . ?" can be monumental. Once you've been able to escape the ruts within your own thinking, amazing things can happen. Often, alternatives will flood your imagination—that is the promise and the product of creative thinking.

Questions Can Clarify a Problem

In the face of an issue or difficulty, have you ever been unclear as to the essence of the problem? Questions can help you pinpoint the root cause. They can help you move past the surface indicators and ensure you are addressing the underlying cause. If your problem is even slightly misdiagnosed, your solutions will miss the mark, and you will not see the outcomes you desire. You get no credit for doing the wrong things well.

Questions Can Help Solve Your Most Challenging Problems

Once you have your problem defined, the fun begins. Now you and your team have the opportunity to solve it. There are many problem-solving models and tools in the world. All the ones I've used will work if you use them well. Questions transcend and permeate most problem-solving approaches. The most blatant use of questions in problem solving is the five-why approach included in the list of new quality management tools. When faced with a nonconformance (problem), ask, "Why?" Upon receiving the answer, ask why a second time, and then a third time—you can see where this is going. The premise is simple—once you get five levels deep, you are usually approaching the truth about the root cause of the problem.

Questions Are a Hedge against Irrelevance

We live in a big world. Although some say it is getting smaller every day, I think it is getting bigger—more knowledge, more opportunity, more reach, more complexity, more choices, and so on. Questions can help us grow with the world, stay connected, and maintain relevance. When we ask thoughtful questions, it grows our heads, hearts, and our spirits of curiosity.

PUTTING YOUR QUESTIONS TO WORK

As far as I know, there is no universally accepted list of the various types of questions. A quick Google search reveals dozens of such lists. Therefore, I've taken the liberty to create one more. This list is not as important as the idea it underscores—you can use questions in countless ways. A well-crafted and thoughtful question can be just what you need in many situations. Questions are a leader's Swiss Army knife; there's a blade for almost everything. Here's my shot at several different applications when a good question may be just what you need.

Communications. If you have been asked to do a presentation, there are some questions that can help you prepare and increase your odds of success.

- Who is in the audience?
- What is the theme of the event?
- Who will speak before me?
- Who will speak after me?
- What is the objective of my presentation?
- What does the audience already know about the topic?
- What do they know about me?
- Who will introduce me?
- What type of media/technology support will be available?
- How will the room be arranged?
- How would I explain the premise of my talk to a small child?
- What do I want the audience to know, feel, and do after the presentation?
- What props, visuals, or activities would reinforce my key point and raise audience engagement?
- What would need to happen for the person who invited me to feel like my presentation was a success?
- How could you convey this information without saying a word?
- How could this message be communicated visually?

Strategy/Planning. A good working definition of strategy is your chosen path to a predetermined goal. With this as our starting point, here are some questions that may help you build a credible plan.

- What do we want to be true in a decade that is not true today?
- What is our current competitive advantage? How can we sustain it? How can we enhance it?

- What are our strengths? How can we leverage them?
- What are the most pressing threats we will face as a team/organization over the next twelve months? Thirty-six months? Sixty months?
- What do we think our competitors are working on? Why would we care?
- What is our time horizon for this planning cycle?
- What are our three to five overarching goals for the next year? Five years?
- Who will serve as our champion for each goal?
- What are our key strategies for each goal/objective?
- What tactics will be required to bring the strategies to life?
- How will we generate buy-in for the plan?
- How will we communicate the plan across the team/organization?
- Who is accountable for plan communications?
- How well have we executed our current plan?
- What will we need to do to execute at a higher level on future plans?
- What does our plan scorecard look like?
- When will we review the plan for progress?
- How will we celebrate our success?

Problem-Solving. The right questions can help with both defining and solving a problem. The next time you or your team is about to begin tackling a problem, try some of these questions.

- What is the presenting problem? By the way, the presenting problem is rarely the real problem.
- What does the data reveal about this problem?
- What is the most expansive way to state the problem?

- What is the narrowest, most pinpointed way we can express the problem?
- What are potential root causes of this problem?
- Which of these potential causes is most likely the primary cause?
- What do the people closest to the problem say about it?
- What has already been tried, if anything, to solve this problem?
- How have others successfully solved this problem?
- If we hired an outside consulting firm to solve this, what do we think they would do?
- What metrics will we use to determine the effectiveness of our intervention(s)?
- Who is responsible for implementing our recommended action plan?

Discovery. This is a broad category of open-ended questions to aid in exploration. You can use them in numerous situations. Try some of these the next time you are planning your vacation, looking for a book to read, or shopping for Christmas gifts.

- What are the options?
- What are the possibilities?
- What are the boundaries?
- What are the nonnegotiables?
- What are my preferences?
- What are the preferences of others?
- What has worked in the past?
- What has failed in the past? Why?
- If time and money were not an issue, what would the right answer be?
- Why are we doing what we are doing?

- What happens if we do nothing?
- How would the situation change if we only had twelve hours to prepare?
- How would the situation change if we had twelve months to prepare?
- If we crowdsourced this issue, what would the general population suggest?
- Can we crowdsource this?
- What else, if anything, have we ever addressed that was similar? What worked in that situation and what did not? Why and why not?

Stimulating (Creativity) Questions. There is a long tradition of using questions in the midst of creative sessions to free our minds and stimulate ideas. I'm sure hundreds of thousands of questions have been used for this same purpose. Here are some for your reference.

- What would the opposite indicate?
- What happens if we make it smaller?
- What happens if we make it bigger?
- How would the most creative person solve this?
- How can we break the problem, and potentially the solution, down into its elemental parts?
- How would you approach this situation if you had an unlimited budget?
- How would you approach this situation if you had *no* budget?

Often these stimulating questions can border on the bizarre. When they do, you may think they will never add any value. Sometimes they do, and sometimes they don't. One fun example is from a session I facilitated when we were discussing how to successfully onboard a new person. The question was "How would you do this underwater?" You can't get much crazier than that.

The conversation that followed included: You don't go scuba diving without a buddy—let's be sure every new person has a buddy. You don't go scuba diving without a predive checklist—let's prepare an onboarding checklist of things that need to happen before the first dive (day). Before we were finished, there were several good ideas sparked by our crazy question.

If you are up for an unorthodox brainstorming session, try some of these stimulating questions.

- How would we solve this on the moon?
- How would this problem have been addressed two hundred years ago?
- How might this problem be solved two hundred years from now?
- If we assume the role of an inanimate object connected to the problem, what solution would we recommend?
- How would a child solve this problem?

Interview Questions. To quote Peter Drucker again, "The most important decision a leader makes is who does what." If you believe this, and even if you debate his conclusion regarding "most important," the interview becomes a pivotal moment in your career as much as the candidate's. Even with the advent of more project-based interviewing, group interviewing, and simulations in the interview process, at the end of the day, we still need to have hardworking questions for the candidate. Here are some favorites from famous people.[1] I'll close this section with one of my own.

- *"What didn't you get a chance to include on your résumé?"* Richard Branson, CEO, The Virgin Group [1]
- *"On a scale of one to ten, how weird are you?"* Tony Hsieh, founder and former CEO, Zappos [1]
- *"How would you describe yourself in one word?"* Dara Richardson-Heron, CEO of YWCA [1]

- *"What would someone who doesn't like you say about you?"* retired general Stanley McChrystal [1]
- *"What did you do to prepare for this interview?"* Suzy Welch, author and speaker [1]
- *"Why would you want to work for . . . you?"* Jack Welch, former CEO, General Electric [1]
- *"What do you want to be when you grow up?"* Stewart Butterfield, founder, Flickr and Slack [1]
- *"What's your dream job?"* Jeff Weiner, CEO, LinkedIn [1]
- *"Why are you here?"* Jack Dorsey, CEO, Twitter [1]
- *"So, what's your story?"* Brian Chesky, CEO, Airbnb [1]

Now, it's my turn. I wanted to include a small break to avoid putting my question alongside Jack Welch, Richard Branson, and the like. One of my favorite interview questions is:

What questions do you have for me?

I believe you can learn so much about someone based on *their* questions. If they don't have any or they are clearly practicing their improv skills in their response, I probably don't have any more questions for them.

ASK BETTER QUESTIONS

Much has been written about asking outstanding questions. Read all you can find and consider making the quest for the right questions a lifelong pursuit. Here are a few tips to jump-start your practice.

Open versus Closed Questions

A question that leads someone to answer with a single word is a closed-ended question, for example, "Did you go to college?" As a general rule, the better way to ask that question and learn more would be to ask an open-ended question—one that invites a more complete response: "What did you do after high school?" In this second, open-ended example, you may learn about a gap-year program in which the interviewee served in an emerging country or hiked the Appalachian Trail. One more thought—if you have to ask if the person went to college, you obviously didn't look at their résumé. Remember: they are sizing you up as well—be prepared.

Single-Barrel versus Multibarrel Questions

I learned this term from Jeff Swatsky. He was the first "question expert" I ever met. At one point, Jeff was traveling the globe, teaching journalists how to ask better questions. He told us the right next question is singular—a *single* question. He showed us video after video of professional journalists asking two, three, or more questions in a single query. These he termed double-barrel or multibarrel questions (I assume after a double-barrel shotgun). The fundamental problem with this approach is twofold: people almost always answer *only* the last question, and in many cases, the last question was not the best question. Single-barrel questions are the best; you can always come back with another.

Leading Questions

I guess these may have a place in editorial journalism, but I don't see them serving leaders very well. In these situations, the person asking the question isn't really trying to discover the other person's point of view. He or she is trying to steer the recipient to a predetermined answer. This is more a technique of advocacy than true inquiry. The reason I include this here is to remind you: Don't use leading questions if you are truly interested in learning something.

SOME OF MY FAVORITE QUESTIONS

I am always looking for a better question. And as we established above, different types of questions serve different purposes.

However, having been a student of this topic for a long time, I still find myself going back to some tried and true questions that have served me well. Here is my *current* list of favorites:

For the Team

- *What specifically are we trying to accomplish?*
- *What do we want to be true in a decade that is not true today?*
- *What one thing could we do in the next ninety days that would have the most impact?*

During a Curiosity Conversation (the topic of our next chapter)

- *What has been your greatest insight in your career thus far?*
- *What advice do you have for me?*
- *Which books have had the biggest impact on your life and career?*
- *How can I serve you?*

For Me

- *How can I add value for this person?*
- *How can I add the most value in this situation?*
- *What did I learn today?*

Questions are in ample supply. And they are free. They work for everyone—rich, poor, young, old, underresourced, affluent, educated, and not. Once you have made the Smart Choice to Fuel Curiosity, you are going to need questions in your toolbox if you want to escape the quicksand and scale your impact.

BE SMART!

Make a list of your favorite questions; three or four will be enough for this activity. If you don't have any favorites, pick a few from the chapter and write them down (or put them in a note on your phone). See how many times you can use these go-to questions over the course of the next week. See what you learn.

Also, if you want bonus points, I would love for you to compile your top-ten questions list and send it to me at Mark@Smart LeadershipBook.com.

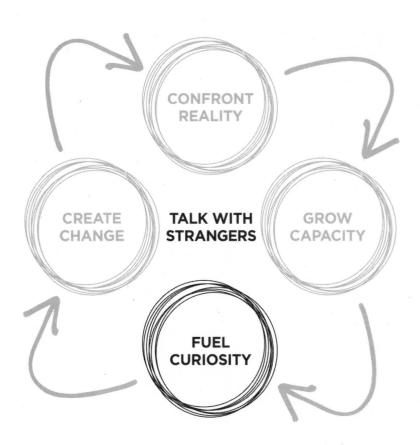

TALK WITH STRANGERS

"Wisdom is the reward you get for a lifetime
of listening when you would have rather talked."
Mark Twain

Do you know the name Brian Grazer? You may not, but you do know his work. He has produced several billion dollars' worth of Hollywood blockbusters including *Apollo 13*, *A Beautiful Mind*, *Splash*, *American Gangster*, and many more. I believe Grazer's book *A Curious Mind*[1] should be required reading for leaders. In it, Grazer attributes his success to his curiosity for sure but mostly to another practice that has fueled his career—he calls them curiosity conversations.

I began this practice decades ago; while I didn't call them curiosity conversations, I just looked for every opportunity to talk with strangers. As you read this chapter, suspend your memories of your mom or dad giving you strict instructions *not* to talk to strangers. If you can overcome this lifelong prohibition, you may find it one of the most productive strategies to Fuel Curiosity and ultimately scale your impact.

Let's go back to Grazer's story. It is a fascinating case study of someone who pushed my thinking on this topic well beyond my experience.

Early in Brian's career in Hollywood, he set a goal to talk to someone in the entertainment industry he did not know *every day*. Over time, he has scaled back his conversations to at least two of these conversations per month. While, early on, his focus was within the motion picture world, he has since broadened his interests to include some of the world's more accomplished people. Now, his conversations exclusively target people *not* in his industry. Brian's story is inspiring to me on several levels—not the least of which is his consistency. He has been having these conversations for thirty-five years.

The list of women and men Brian has talked to over the years is stunning—an extremely diverse who's who list including some of the most famous people in the world from all disciplines and many other names you and I would never recognize. He has had conversations with Muhammad Ali, Margaret Thatcher, Andy Warhol, Oprah Winfrey, E. O. Wilson, Jonas Salk, Ronald Reagan, Prince, Wolfgang Puck, John McCain, Jim Lovell, Calvin Klein, Shelia Johnson, Jacques Cousteau, and hundreds more.

WHO DO YOU WANT TO TALK TO?

If you are a seasoned leader with a strong, decades-long, and deep network, you probably have access to scores of interesting people. However, if you are early in your career, your starting place is different—and that's okay. My encouragement to you is to start where you are. Even a few intentional conversations could launch a lifelong practice.

Regardless of your starting point, you will still want to be somewhat selective. Here are some filters you can use to begin the process. As you look at these different categories, I encourage you to jot down a few names for each one as they come to mind.

People Who Do What You Do Better Than You Do

Think about what you do for a living. Think about your key roles within your job description. Make a list of people who are extremely good at the specific activities you want to improve upon. I have two specific coaching points to offer.

First, it is good to aim high. You can begin taking steps to connect with women and men who are giants in your field. However, because the odds are lower that you can meet with them in the near future, my second bit of advice is to create a second, more attainable list. These people should still be better than you—but they don't have to be rock stars in your field. I would guess, over the years, 80 percent of my talks with strangers have *not* been with superstars, but every conversation has still added value.

People Who Will Stretch Your Thinking

Pursuing conversations with people who will stretch your thinking is always a good idea. Maybe this is someone who has a global perspective while your worldview is more national or regional. Maybe this is someone who has a reputation for innovation. Perhaps this individual has changed careers, industries, or organizations several times and therefore has a perspective you do not. Maybe this person has a reputation for being creative, strategic, or getting results, and you want to learn and be challenged in one of these areas.

People Who Work in Other Disciplines

This is where these conversations may take on a little more risk, and the potential for reward increases. If you want to learn more about closing a sale and meet with someone who is really good at this, the boundaries and expectations of the conversation are clear, if not explicit. However, we don't know what we don't know. If you are in manufacturing, you don't know what you might learn from a conversation with a surgeon. If you are a private sector leader, the lessons to be gleaned from a nonprofit leader are perhaps less clear. This doesn't mean you should avoid these conversations. On the contrary, new ideas, insights, and innovation are often born when women and men from different disciplines invest time together.

People Who Have Different Worldviews

How much time do you intentionally spend with people who see the world differently than you do? The options include, but are not limited to, different races, political parties, faith traditions, socioeconomic levels, educational backgrounds, stages of life, nationalities, and people who grew up in other countries. What will you learn from these people? I don't know, and neither do you. We'll talk more later in this chapter about preparation for your talk with a stranger.

Smart People

Obviously, there is likely overlap in these categories. However, I wanted to call attention to this one because it has been a go-to for me throughout my career. Someone asked me, "How would you describe your approach to work?"

I loved this question. Here's what I came up with in the moment: "My approach to work is to gather the smartest people I can find around the table and go to work together to accomplish whatever needs to be done." It is an offshoot of that approach that prompts this category of conversations—sometimes you can't get everyone "around the table," but you can still talk to people. One of my filters if I am thinking about a particular topic is "Who are the smartest people I know who could add value to a conversation on a particular topic?"

HOW DO YOU GAIN AN AUDIENCE?

Start with People You Know

Remember, you are generally looking for people who are willing to have a conversation with you about a topic you are both interested in, and they fit in one or more of the categories listed. You already know some of these people. Granted, it might be a tangential relationship or maybe you just swapped contact info at a party. I would start with these people. I'm guessing there is a deep well of information already in your contacts.

Leverage Existing Relationships

After you have a list of conversations you want to schedule, begin to contact your network. Even if the people you know don't know the people you want to talk with, they may know someone who does. "Do you know XYZ?" Or, "Who do you know that might know them?" All you are looking for initially are introductions; some of these will turn into conversations.

Seize Unexpected Opportunities

When I attended TED several years ago, Dr. Edward de Bono was one of the speakers. If you don't know Dr. de Bono, he is a former Rhodes Scholar who taught at Oxford, Cambridge, Harvard, and London College, holds several degrees, including a PhD in medicine, has written eighty-five books, and is one of the leading thinkers on the topic of creativity. I had read some of de Bono's books and taught his content on more than one occasion. This felt like an opportunity I didn't want to miss. So, after his talk, I approached him and asked if I could buy him a meal while he was in the States. He said yes!

On the way to lunch, he told me that in a recent auction, someone had paid $25,000 for dinner with him. I told him my Amex might not cover $25,000, but I would be delighted to pay for the meal. We had a wonderful, thought-provoking, two-hour lunch.

Not all my attempts have been successful, but that's okay with me. You never know if you don't ask. When an opportunity presents itself, seize it.

Ask for Recommendations

This is an easy, often overlooked way to find and meet interesting people—ask for suggestions and recommendations. This can be especially helpful if you already know people in your area of interest. Asking for suggestions and recommendations for others to talk to can sometimes be a helpful question near the end of your conversations. "Who else do you think I should talk to about   ? Would you be willing to make an introduction?"

HOW DO YOU MAXIMIZE THE TIME?

If you consider the time you have with the person a gift, you will want to steward the time well. Here are some quick tips on how to get ready.

Prepare

You have to decide what level of preparation is necessary. However, if you are in doubt, overprepare. This accomplishes several things: your preparation communicates the value you place on the time together. This could work in your favor if you want a second meeting. Advance preparation also helps you identify specific areas you want to explore (e.g., "Dr. de Bono, can you please help me understand how to fight my natural bias toward vertical thinking?" Or, "In *Six Thinking Hats*, when you talked about the risk of rushing toward the Blue Hat, can you tell me more about the risks?"). Advance prep also helps you use your time wisely. More on crafting some discussion questions in a moment. Finally, advance preparation will help you move the person you are talking with off script.

Try to Get Them off the Script

The more expertise and experience someone has, the harder it will be to get them off script. We all have scripts, especially if we have been asked about a topic many times before. Back to the recommendation about preparation. If you know someone's answer to your questions from their writing, speeches, podcast, or other channels, don't go there. You should be attempting to move the conversation beyond their previous responses and learn something you cannot find in their published work.

If someone has just published a book on five keys to happiness, you might get them off script by asking about the sixth: "When you were writing the five keys, I'm sure you considered many other 'keys'; if you were going to include a sixth key, what would it be?" Wait for their answer (no double-barrel questions). Depending on their response, a good follow-up question might be, "Why did you ultimately decide to exclude it from the book?" Now you are off script. Will anything of value come of it? Maybe, maybe not. Occasionally, you will discover gold when you are off the beaten trail. When working with an expert, don't waste their time or yours getting a book report. Just read their book(s) (preferably in advance).

Have a Clear Objective

This is a little bit tricky and subject to a real-time decision on your part. To secure a meeting, you are probably going to need to tell the person why you want to meet. I take very few meetings without clarity on the topic, and I'm not famous—just a guy trying to use my time wisely. So you need to have something in mind. My suggestion is to keep it broad but directional (e.g., "Dr. de Bono, I've read several of your books, and I'm interested to learn more about how leaders can be more creative."). This is not to say you might not talk about other topics during your time together. Having a primary objective will also help you craft some good questions.

Ask Good Questions—But Don't Be Bound by Them

There is art and science on this one. I have already invested a previous chapter on the power of questions. Here are a couple of additional tips. One, create more questions than you think you'll have time to ask and put them in some order or sequence *based on priority*. I heard an interview once in which the person conducting the interview only asked one question and the person being interviewed talked for about twenty minutes. The interview was over. The good news: the first question was brilliant, and so was the response. I'm glad the first question was a good one. Two, use the questions you walk in with as a starting point for the conversation. Do not feel compelled to ask them all. You get no points for getting through your questions. There is something better.

Pursue Open Doors

I have already mentioned the courses I recently completed on ethnographic interviewing. This idea of pursuing open doors was probably my biggest takeaway from two quarters of work. If our initial queries are positioned carefully, the person we are talking with will often open doors for us to go through if we are attentive and open to the possibilities. Behind these doors, we often find a fresh perspective, new thought, or something we would have never discovered if we moved doggedly through our questions. Imagine this snippet from a longer conversation.

> **Q:** What's your definition of leadership?
> **A:** Well, I've been thinking about that a lot recently. I guess my answer is blah, blah, blah.

Rather than thinking, *Check, I have her definition of leadership*, what else might you learn if you followed her response with something else:

> **Follow-up Question:** Thanks, that was helpful. Can we go back? You said you've been thinking about this a lot recently—what have you been thinking?
> **A:** I've been thinking about the challenges of leadership.

Q: Which challenges?

A: Primarily the tension between results and relationships.

Q: Is there a story from your life you can share to help me better understand this tension?

You see how the person opened a door? All I had to do was recognize it and ask an appropriate follow-up question. Keep your questions handy but don't hesitate to go off script. That's where the really good stuff is often hiding.

Take Good Notes (or Record the Session)

Early in my career I missed this one. I was shortsighted and really didn't understand the long-term value of some of the conversations I had an opportunity to have. Today, I take much better notes, and depending on the circumstances, sometimes I ask for permission to record the conversation. We interviewed scores of leaders for this book—we recorded almost all of them. Knowing that we will have the recording and the transcription allows me to be more focused in the conversation. I find it difficult to take copious notes in the midst of a conversation. Another advantage of recording the conversation: more than once, I've gone back to my notes and found them insufficient. I knew there was a quote or a story I had not fully captured or was missing critical details.

Also, when taking notes in real time as my only means of capturing the wisdom in the room, I do not recognize as many of the open doors we just discussed—I am too distracted trying to get it all down.

One more idea that can sometimes be appropriate: you may want to enlist a partner to be in the conversation with you. One of you can focus more on carrying the conversation and looking for those open doors while the other can be more focused on documenting the conversation.

WHAT HAPPENS AFTER THE CONVERSATION?

Process Your Conversation

You would likely do this without my prompting, but let's just consider it a friendly reminder. I would suggest you schedule time with yourself after the session to process what you heard. This part of the process will vary based on the situation, but I find it helpful to fill in any gaps in my notes, record any observations not yet documented, synthesize your big takeaways, identify insights, and confirm any action items.

Attempt to Incorporate Something You Learned

Before I describe this practice, I want to freely admit what I'm suggesting here is not always possible, nor is it the primary reason you had the conversation in the first place. However, if you can pull it off, it will probably enhance your leadership and may even give you additional energy for your next conversation.

Years ago, while leading our quality and customer satisfaction team, benchmarking was all the rage. If you are not familiar with the concept, simply stated, it is the practice of visiting an organization who does something you do better than you do it, for the purpose of improving your team's performance.

As I was learning about this quality-improvement strategy, I was challenged by the idea that if you did not incorporate something you learned during your visit, your benchmarking effort would be deemed unsuccessful. Failure to incorporate some best practice was thought of as "industrial tourism," not real benchmarking. This nuance has served as a valuable reminder and encouragement for me as I've had a chance to benchmark many of the world's best organizations. "What can I *apply* from this visit?" is never a bad question.

As it relates to your conversations, "What can I apply from the conversation?" is also never a bad question. I share this question to set the bar high. As I said, sometimes there will be no immediate application from your conversation—that's okay, but if you are looking for application, you are more likely to find it.

Share Your Experience

I offer this suggestion for three reasons—none of these will surprise you. One, you've probably heard the expression "The best way to learn something is to teach it." Well, I'm not sure that's true, but teaching something does force you to synthesize learnings, articulate key takeaways, and codify your insights.

Next, if you invest the time and energy in these conversations, sharing your experience represents better stewardship. Allowing others to benefit from your opportunity increases the probability of impact.

Finally, you can use your conversations as a catalyst for other conversations and action. Imagine the impact you can have as you intentionally help others learn, grow, and apply the lessons you were exposed to. These secondary conversations may also spark someone else to embrace this practice of talking with strangers.

Follow Up

What you do here is totally up to you. However, you do need to do something. It could be as simple as sending a handwritten note that says thanks or sending a copy of a book the two of you discussed. During one of my conversations for this project, someone recommended a book to me they believed would be helpful. I bought it, read it, and sent a note thanking him, letting him know I took his advice. If someone has been generous with their time, regardless of your method of choice, follow up.

One additional idea: What I just described, I consider immediate follow-up within seven to ten days. You can also follow up weeks and months later. If you find a podcast, a book, or an article that pertains to what you discussed, send them a copy. If you are going to be in their city, you can offer to buy them a meal. If you learn he or she is going to be in your city, ask them how you can serve them during their stay—restaurant recommendations, hotels, transportation, and the like.

BE SMART!

Have you made it your practice to intentionally talk with strangers on a regular basis? If not, why not give it a try? Be bold and attempt to schedule one conversation next month. See what happens; see what you can learn. My guess is this could be one of your favorite strategies to make good on your choice to Fuel Curiosity.

SMART CHOICE #4

**CREATE
CHANGE**

CREATE CHANGE

"The best way to predict the future is to invent it."
Peter Drucker

One day in 1984, while watching the Olympics, Ruben Gonzalez decided he too wanted to be an Olympian. On the surface, there were several problems with his newfound dream. First, he had no particular sport in mind nor was he predisposed to either summer or winter sports. By his own admission, he was not an athletically inclined guy. The next problem was one of timing. Countless others around the world had embraced similar dreams. However, the rare air of the Olympics is typically enjoyed by young people who have invested much of their childhood pursuing this opportunity—Ruben was a twenty-one-year-old copier salesman living in Houston, Texas.

Ruben first considered the Summer Games and realized there were no sports he could strive for—he could not run fast or jump high. Not to be dissuaded, Ruben shifted his focus to the Winter Games. After doing some research, Ruben narrowed his focus to the following: ski jump, bobsled, and luge. He was particularly intrigued by the luge when he learned that 90 percent of the people who begin training for this event quit. *Fabulous*, he thought. *I just won't quit.*

After what he describes as a series of difficult conversations, Ruben finally convinced the folks who ran the program to allow him to train at the facility in Lake Placid. As Ruben describes the first two years of his training, he says he was crashing eight out of every ten runs. He broke multiple bones and was "sponsored" by MasterCard, because he was charging all his expenses on his personal credit card! And then, in 1988, the unthinkable happened. Ruben made the Olympic Team.

Even more unbelievable than the fact Ruben is an Olympian at all, he has now competed in *four* Winter Games in four different decades!

One of the lesser-known facets of Ruben's story was his debilitating fear of the luge. Each time he made it to the bottom of the track, it would take up to twenty minutes to convince himself to do it again. He said he "white-knuckled it" for twenty-five years. The reason he continued: The luge was the vehicle to his dream of participating in the Olympics.

While Ruben was training for his *fourth* Olympics, a coach finally helped him overcome his fear. The trick, as it was described to Ruben, was to shift his focus from his immediate surroundings to a point in front of the sled. The walls and the speed were indeed fear-inducing, but focusing on the way forward, the coach promised, would be freeing. It worked; his fear was gone. Ruben is now attempting to make the US team again in 2022 and become the oldest Olympian in the modern era—he will be sixty years old when the world gathers in Beijing.

Think about your story. Have you done something that couldn't be done, something that had never been done before? Have you accomplished anything others said was impossible?

Maybe you were the first in your family to go to college. Perhaps you started your own business. Maybe you overcame a dire diagnosis. Maybe you decided to run a marathon when you had never run a mile in your life—and you did it. Did you invest in someone in whom you saw potential when no one else did only to see that bet pay off? Have you ever helped a team or organization accomplish a bold and ambitious objective? I'm assuming one or more of these things is true of you. At some point in your life, you have beaten the odds, defied conventional wisdom, and prevailed. Just like Ruben, you have chosen to Create Change.

Sometimes the change is private and personal; in other cases, it is very public. Sometimes you are leading yourself, and sometimes you are leading others. In either case, leaders Create Change. This is the fourth Smart Choice the best leaders make repeatedly. It is also the pivotal choice when trying to escape the quicksand that impedes our effectiveness.

THE SMART CHOICE

Create Change today to ensure a better tomorrow.

As a student and practitioner of leadership for more than four decades, I cannot count the times I have been asked about the definition of leadership. As our research revealed decades ago, there are literally thousands of published definitions. As I reflect on my evolving responses over the years, I stand by all of them. However, I always reserve the right to get smarter.

Although there are many perfectly acceptable definitions of leadership, and I'm sure many more will be written in the years to come, this Smart Choice captures the essence of leadership better than I've previously been able to articulate—the ability to Create Change is at the heart of true leadership.

What is it leaders do? Leaders around the world cast vision, build teams, allocate resources, and so on. Of course they do. But *why*? To what end?

What is the ultimate test of a leader? Some would ask, "Did he or she create a better future? Did the leader create positive change?" If the answer to either of these questions is yes, I can tell you at least one thing they certainly did: these women and men made a choice to Create Change.

Leaders understand to their core that they are ultimately accountable for their ability to channel the resources, activities, hearts, and minds of people to create a better tomorrow.

I don't want to dwell on this since it may be obvious, but I want to share what for me was an insight. I see many leaders stuck in action (translated: they are busy but not going anywhere) because they are unwilling to embrace this fundamental idea: leaders are *supposed* to Create Change.

If leadership is about helping people and organizations move toward a preferred future, swimming in quicksand is not only *not* helpful, it forces a leader to actually forfeit the opportunity to lead. You cannot lead while stuck in the status quo. Progress is the promise of leadership.

If creating positive change is our job, what blocks so many would-be leaders from making this choice? In many cases, it's not that they couldn't master the skills required for leadership; for some, the obstacle lives much deeper in their subconsciousness.

The prerequisite to the crucial and essential choice to Create Change is a belief in one's own agency. Is it even possible for an individual to create the future? For the most effective leaders, the answer is a resounding yes!

USE THE FORCE

Even if you have never watched the Star Wars movies, you are probably aware of the special power possessed by some of the characters—the Force, as it is called, is a mysterious source of strength, insight, and untold abilities. But there's a catch—Luke Skywalker and others must learn to "use the Force," a gift of unknown origin that comes without an instruction manual. As legend has it, the Jedi are the keepers of this ancient Force.

In today's world, leaders are the keepers of a very similar power—a source of strength, insight, and untold abilities, including the ability to see the unseen and create the future. We too must learn to channel and use this force. This chapter will introduce you to the two sources of your power; like a pair of nuclear reactors residing deep in your spirit, they provide an ever-ready source of energy for good in the world: an internal locus of control and a growth mindset.

Henry Ford said, "Whether you think you can or think you can't—you're right." He was right. This is the essence of locus of control. It may sound like a quip from the positive psychology movement—but it's so much more. We embrace a pattern of thought, and our thoughts shape our actions; and of course, our actions, or lack thereof, shape our outcomes. Leaders who don't believe they can successfully Create Change will be reluctant to attempt to do so. The attempt to Create Change is a wonderful, challenging, sometimes frustrating, often bewildering adventure—and it is a choice.

If this is a new concept for you, you may be wondering, "Doesn't every leader have an internal locus of control?" The short answer is no. Some people have an external locus of control.

If you draw a continuum with "My Actions *Do* Impact Outcomes" on one end and "My Actions Do *Not* Impact Outcomes" on the other, you can plot a person's general worldview on this line. Those who believe they have a high degree of influence on events are labeled as having an internal locus of control. Those who see events and circumstances as beyond their influence and in the control of others are the group with an external locus of control.

LOCUS OF CONTROL

INTERNAL   **EXTERNAL**

"My Actions *Do*   "My Actions Do *Not*
Impact Outcomes."   Impact Outcomes."

Even if you've never heard of these terms before, you can begin to see the implications for your leadership. For now, let's assume you want to strengthen your internal locus of control. Here's how.

Decide to Change Your Thinking

If you want to modify your thinking, you can, but first, you must decide to change. This may sound like an obvious first step, but as with many other things in life, meaningful, positive change begins with a decision. You don't drift to a better place—you make a decision and go to work. You must behave your way to a better future—you don't hope yourself there.

Select Your Next Project

At some point, an internal locus of control will become an unconscious bias: you won't have to think about it. However, while developing this way of seeing your role in the world, it will require conscious focus. One way to do this is to select a test case or a project. This can be large or small, but it is probably more prudent if you start small. Examples include solving a problem at work, learning a new skill, getting stronger physically, memorizing a poem or piece of literature, or taking up a new hobby. All of these require some diligence and should be achievable.

Focus on What You Can Control

In any endeavor, there are elements you control and ones you do not. Understanding the difference is a worthwhile effort. Then, be sure to apply your energy to the items you control. Let's take a sticky example. If someone treated you poorly in the past, restoring this relationship could be one of your projects, but you have to be careful. You do not control how someone else responds—you do control your actions. In this case, try forgiving them for treating you poorly. This is what you can do. It will be liberating, and you will realize it was *your action* that created the impact. That's what an internal locus of control is all about. *You* can make a difference.

Identify Specific Actions

Given a specific project or objective and identifying what you can control are good steps, but to really make progress, you need to identify specific actions you can take and do it. Several years ago, my son suggested we run a marathon. Because I had never run to the mailbox, I had to identify specific, concrete actions I could take. Hope is not a strategy. I had to do some things if I was going to succeed. These included buying a book (I highly recommend the *Non-Runner's Marathon Trainer* by Kole, Whitsett, and Dolgener) and purchasing some shoes.

So far, so good, but at some point, I had to start running. Hold on. The book suggested I start slowly and contained a walking plan that slowly increased to a running plan. Remember baby steps? I took them—all the recommended steps were within my control. The result: we did it—I finished the race.

Learn from Your Mistakes

This is a strategy that can be extremely profitable. If we are keenly aware of our mistakes, we can take steps to avoid them in the future. This requires some discipline and some time, but it is a wise investment. The deliberate act of avoiding the same mistake twice is empirical evidence you do have some level of control over your outcomes.

As painful as this sounds, I would suggest you invest time in documenting your mistakes—call them "lessons learned" if it makes you feel any better. The more precise you can be, the better—document where you went wrong and, equally important, take good notes on why you missed the mark. Granted, sometimes the answer will not be obvious. Just beware: if you can't pinpoint the reason for the misstep, the chances are high you'll make the same mistake again.

Repeat the Process—Forever

Take on your next project, make a difference, and when you do, your confidence will grow. Gradually raise your sights and take on bigger projects, maybe even with increasing risk levels. When you fall short, get up and try again. You will succeed more than you will fail. My prediction is you will become addicted to creating positive change in your world.

A GROWTH MINDSET

Perhaps the Force is not naturally strong in you like it was in Luke Skywalker. Are you out of luck as a leader? Certainly not! This is where a growth mindset, an idea popularized in recent years by Carol Dweck out of Stanford University, comes into play.[1]

A growth mindset is the belief that you can continue to learn and grow throughout your lifetime, and this growth is the by-product of dedication and hard work. The opposing worldview is what she labels a fixed mindset—what is just is. If you are not smart, you are out of luck; if you are not a good communicator, too bad; if you cannot lead, move out of the way and let a "natural" leader step up.

According to an article by Tchiki Davis published in *Psychology Today*, individuals with a fixed mindset also have a tendency to shy away from projects requiring extra effort or those with higher levels of risk.[2] They also avoid making mistakes. You can see why a fixed mindset is catastrophic for a leader—all of the attributes you need to Create Change and build a better tomorrow will be compromised if you allow a fixed mindset to persist.

The overarching positive implications for us as leaders are huge and full of opportunity. If the Force is not particularly strong in you—if you tend to think forces out of your control have rendered you a victim of some cosmic roulette game and you are just waiting to see if your winning number ever comes up—you can change the game. But you must have a growth mindset. As a leader, your growth mindset is the permission slip to learn, grow, and create the future for the rest of your life.

LET THE TRAINING BEGIN

A belief in your ability to grow, or not, probably has deep roots. As a child, well-meaning parents, teachers, coaches, and other authority figures began programming you through the messages you repeatedly heard. These included "Good job," "Great work," "You're getting better," "That's not right," "You're never going to get this right," "Why can't you learn?" "Your sister understands this," and other less direct but nonetheless nonverbal and symbolic gestures. We can't unpack those here. Let's just admit you're a complex product of many, many factors. Add to this your natural temperament, wiring, personality, and strengths, and you have you.

So our objective in this section is to help you accept your past but not be bound by it. Hopefully, some of the following ideas will help you believe in your ability to grow.

Commit to Grow—Don't Try

As young Luke was training in the swamp with Yoda, the Jedi master, he was struggling. The discipline required, the ability to believe in himself, the fear of failure and the unknown, combined with general doubt about his abilities, were so strong that he was having trouble unleashing the Force within him. At one point of frustration and exhaustion, he tells Yoda, "I'm trying."

Yoda's response is my word for you: "Try not! Do or do not. There is no try." For some of you, this is the key that will unlock your futures as leaders.

Remember Your Purpose

Change is hard in any domain, but to change the way you see the world is incredibly difficult. One of the primary sustainable drivers of human motivation is a strong sense of purpose. As Simon Sinek has popularized in recent years, start with why. If you haven't done the deep work of articulating your why, now is the best time to begin. Here are some questions to help jump-start your journey or help you refine what you've already begun:

- Why do you want to cultivate a growth mindset?
- How is your fixed mindset limiting your life and career?
- What would you pursue if you had no fear of failure?
- What would you attempt if your success was ensured?
- If income were of no concern, what would you do and why?
- What do you think you were born to do?
- What do your unique talents, experiences, and passions prepare you to do for the world?
- What do you want to be remembered for?

The seed of your purpose is probably in your answers to these questions. If you want a free resource, "Discover Your Purpose," please go to SmartLeadershipBook.com/Purpose.

Learn from Others' Mistakes

Truett Cathy, the founder of Chick-fil-A, was more than my boss and the man who gave me a chance to become the sixteenth employee in his company; he was a mentor as well. He told me early and often, "You don't have to make all the mistakes yourself. Learn from the mistakes of others." This was sound advice forty years ago, and I would guess it will still be valid forty years from now. If you want to have more of a growth mindset, you need to see your efforts succeed. This will build your confidence. Pay attention to what others are doing—what works and what doesn't. This should inform your actions and help you win more often.

Learn Something Every Day

A growth mindset is fundamentally about the belief that if you put in the effort, you can learn and grow. Extinguish any doubts and thoughts to the contrary by proving yourself wrong. Set a goal to learn something every day; yes, every day. The more you look for something, the more likely you are to find it.

To pull this off, you may need to change your behavior as well as your orientation. Try listening to podcasts or audiobooks during your commute or while you work out. Have a set of ready questions you can ask when you are with others who possess different skill sets or work in different roles. Then, at the end of every day, write down at least one thing you learned that day. At the end of the week, review your learning journal. You can develop a growth mindset.

Share What You Learn

This is a powerful strategy to cultivate a growth mindset. When you commit to share what you are learning, it will change the way you see the world—it will reduce your fear of failure and stimulate your growth. Sharing your learning journey has many other benefits; a few of them were mentioned in the previous chapter. The more you share, the more benefits you will enjoy.

There are countless ways to share what you are learning—one-on-one, in meetings, in presentations, on social media, and more.

Seth Godin says his decision to blog daily is one of his top five career choices. Here's what he said on the Unmistakable Creative Podcast:

> *If you know you have to write a blog post tomorrow, something in writing, something that will be around six months from now, about something in the world, you will start looking for something in the world to write about. You will seek to notice something interesting and to say something creative about it. Well, isn't that all we're looking for? The best practice of generously sharing what you notice about the world is exactly the antidote for your fear.*[3]

Take More Small Risks

If you are not convinced you can learn and grow, one of the unintended consequences is risk aversion. You must beat this fear. The risk itself, and the occasional failure, is when we learn the most.

I recently had an experience I'm sure many of you can relate to. My youngest grandson, Finn, has just learned to walk. Watching him has been a master class in taking increasing levels of risk. In the beginning, he would stand and hold on to something. For him, this was a huge risk. Having spent the first nine or more months on the floor, he is now towering above the toys he used to swim in. However, from the look on his face, the risk paid off. I think he actually loved his new heightened view of the world.

Shortly thereafter, he began to stand more than sit and scoot along the furniture, moving about between the sofa and the coffee table, still holding on. I am sure this newfound mobility was exhilarating and terrifying, but he pressed on.

One day, he let go, and he fell, but he didn't die, so he decided to try it all again. Then, one day, against his better judgment, he let go and took a baby step. You could see the apprehension on his face. *This is crazy!* he must have been thinking. Then he fell again, but he didn't quit. Over the coming days, he took another step and another and another, and then he became a toddler; soon he will be a walker, and one day, he will be a runner. It all started with a risk.

What baby step could you take today?

Celebrate Your Progress

Not to trivialize it, but a growth mindset is a mind game. There may be nothing more important for you to do at this point in your life than to believe you can learn and grow. The challenge is in your head. What you believe about your talent, skills, and ability is under your control.

What controls the way we see the world? Obviously, this is too big a question to really tackle here but one that prompts an idea. One of the ways human beings form their attitudes and beliefs is based on what is affirmed, what is recognized, and what is celebrated. Something I learned from Plato (not personally) applies here: "What is honored in a country is cultivated there."[4]

If you want to cultivate a growth mindset, recognize and reward yourself for the baby steps you take. Celebrate in whatever form or fashion you would like—just don't miss the moment to relish the small wins.

Armed with your newfound or improving growth mindset, the Force will be stronger in you. Use it wisely.

WAITING FOR SUPERMAN

Geoffrey Canada grew up believing in Superman, literally. He recalls the day he learned Superman was just a story: "I was devastated when I realized no one was coming with the power to save us."[5] However, this revelation didn't slow Geoffrey down for long—he decided he would have to save his world himself.

Growing up in the South Bronx, where poverty and crime created a toxic mix, Canada was able to escape through an academic path. He excelled in school and ultimately earned degrees from Bowdoin and Harvard.

Understanding the circumstances of his childhood all too well, Canada made the choice to Create Change when he started the Harlem Children's Zone (HCZ) in 1990. Their stated mission is to increase high school graduation rates and college admissions. They did!

Now, the success of his program reverberates across the globe. In 2014, *Fortune* named Geoffrey one of the top fifty leaders in the world. The *New York Times* called the venture "one of the most ambitious social-policy experiments of our time."[4]

Geoffrey's story is unique for sure, but there is a thread within it that connects every leader who has ever lived. If you have ever envisioned a preferred future and worked to make it happen, you have changed your world too. You may not have received the notoriety Geoffrey has—they made a major motion picture about his efforts called *Waiting for Superman*. Nonetheless, absent the recognition, you should be able to relate to the core of his story. Leadership requires a belief in what can be—what must be. This belief compels leaders to Create Change.

BE SMART!

Identify at least one specific situation or circumstance in your life or leadership in which you want to Create Change, beginning today. Your current reality is not your destiny; it is only a moment in time.

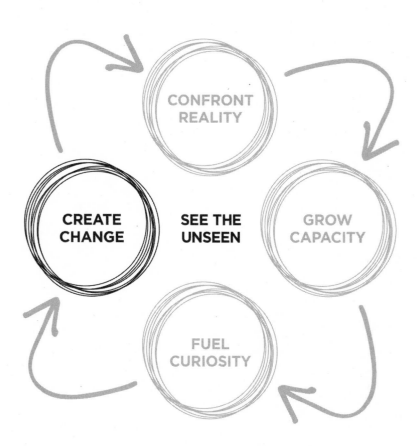

CONFRONT
REALITY

GROW
CAPACITY

FUEL
CURIOSITY

CREATE
CHANGE

SEE THE
UNSEEN

SEE THE UNSEEN

*"The people who are crazy enough to think
they can change the world are the ones who do."*
Steve Jobs

Napoleon Bonaparte is widely held as one of the best generals of all time. Much has been written about his military and strategic prowess. But what really propelled a corporal to an emperor in a matter of a few short years? Historians have differing views as to the source of his genius—no doubt a blend of factors. However, I think one of his defining characteristics was his ability to see the unseen. We see a glimpse of this in the silent film *Napoleon* by Abel Gance, which debuted in Paris in 1927.

In the film, the audience is introduced to then twenty-four-year-old Napoleon during the siege of Tulon in 1793. As he reports for duty, he learns of the general's plans for a frontal attack on the enemy. In the movie, the general asks Napoleon, "If you were in my place, little man, what would you do?"

Napoleon's suggestion is to take the small nearby fort of l'Aiguillete. He contended that once it is taken, the English will leave Tulon for fear of being cut off from their navy.

The general laughs, then proceeds with his plan and is defeated. The next general is open to Napoleon's suggestion, adopts his strategy, and takes the fort. As Napoleon predicted, the English retreat without a battle in Tulon. This victory launches Napoleon's career and his rise to power.

William Duggin, in his book *Strategic Intuition*,[1] tells how Napoleon used this ability to see the unseen over and over again. One notable element of his thought process was on display in his pre-battle routine. Napoleon would ride from point to point surveying potential points of attack. He would envision the assault from that spot and anticipate the outcome. If he could not see his men winning from that spot, he would move to another. He repeated this again and again, to the befuddlement of his officers, until he could "see" a victory. When he did, he would say, "We will attack from here."

What's your favorite part of leadership? Have you thought about it? Leadership is such a broad and complex discipline that your answer could be one of many facets of the role. For some of you, the joy is in building the team; for others, it is solving wicked problems; and for many, the real high comes when the work is completed and you have succeeded. All of these are legitimate responses.

For me, one of my favorite parts of the role is to see what is not yet but needs to be, and then articulate it in such a way that others will rally around it. I think seeing the unseen is a blast. Of course, all the other things have to happen too. If you just see the future and nothing ever happens, you are not a leader, you are a dreamer.

Even if seeing the unseen is not your favorite part of the job, there is something about envisioning a preferred future that is energizing to most leaders. When you and I serve in this role, we are the architects of the future.

WHY VISION MATTERS

First, let's put this facet of our role in context. This book is built on the premise that you and I can make four Smart Choices to scale our impact. The first three Smart Choices have positioned us well to

Create Change. Inherent in this fourth choice is the presumption we know where we want to go. Leadership always begins with a picture of the future. But this is not the only reason vision matters.

Vision Is a Powerful Catalyst for Positive Change

The future is not yet written; it will be written by leaders. We have the opportunity to describe that future in vivid detail. The future we envision will build on the past yet improve upon it. If it were not better, why would we, or anyone, be willing to pursue it?

A well-formed and articulated picture of a preferred future is like a compass for the head and a magnet for the heart. If you help people approach the vision and see why it is, in fact, a good place for them, they will help you create it. By the way, you need them. If the vision is so small you can make it a reality by yourself, why are you trying to rally others?

Vision Provides Direction

When a leader paints a compelling picture of where she or he would like to take people, there is another, less often discussed benefit— they are also telling people what they are not going to do.

When Southwest Airlines set out in 1967 as a regional, low-cost airline serving Texas, this provided unwavering clarity and direction for their organization and shareholders. They were saying they would not pursue the strategy of other airlines—they would be different. This is a good test for your vision; what options does it remove from consideration?

Vision Creates Energy

People love to be part of something bigger than themselves. Vision is the mechanism for leaders to package and transmit a bigger something. A compelling vision stirs people's imaginations, lifts their spirits, and stimulates their thinking. A mind and heart stretching vision is like a turbocharger on a car. It increases horsepower on demand. If your picture of the future is big, really big, you will need every ounce of energy you can muster. Also, as energy inevitably wanes, a fresh shot of vision will be needed to reignite the passion of the organization.

Vision Creates Followers

When a leader takes a step of faith and casts what she believes to be a compelling picture of the future, there is always risk. Is the vision right? Is it too timid? Is it too bold? Is it achievable? Will people buy in? From the leader's perspective, all of these questions are real and consequential. However, ultimate success may have more to do with the question of buy-in than scope, scale, or "rightness of the vision." When a leader declares a destination, some will want to follow, and others will not. That's okay, and it's really good to know who is with you. Don't be surprised, if you articulate an audacious vision, some may choose not to go with you.

Vision Creates Focus

An often missed or undervalued benefit of a clear vision is the focus it creates. I don't need to tell you about all you are facing in your world. If you want some language to describe it, go back and take a look at the chapter on quicksand. Vision can be what my friend and consultant Bobb Biehl calls a "fog cutter." In the midst of all the noise, clutter, distractions, and fog, what is really important? Your answer may not even be singular in light of all you have going on, but the vision should be on your list. What are you doing today to advance the vision?

Vision Informs Strategy

One of the questions I receive from time to time is someone asking me to evaluate a tactic or a batch of tactics. My response is always the same: What is the strategy? In the absence of strategy, every tactic is of equal value. The same logic applies when evaluating strategy. In the absence of a larger objective, goal, or vision, it is impossible to accurately assess the value or potential efficacy of a strategy. If you are clear on the vision, it will help your team create the strategies required to realize your vision. Here's a bonus assignment for you. If you currently have a vision in place, audit your key strategies—how many of them are helping you move closer to your vision?

WHERE DO YOU FIND VISION?

Let's move forward with the assumption you see the wisdom in using vision as a tool to aid you on your journey to Create Change. What's next? If we were sitting down with the cup of coffee I mentioned earlier, I would ask you to share your vision. Let's continue to pretend—suppose you don't have a vision but want one. Here's my advice to you.

Let your imagination, intuition, creativity, experience, insight, and judgment collide. Bring your best thinking to the task at hand. You can create vision at the personal, team, department, division, organization, community, national, or global level.

A word of caution: as you read all of this information regarding vision, please don't assume creating the vision is someone else's role. I see this all the time. Leaders at all levels often defer vision creation to their boss or their boss's boss. If you are a leader, *you* need a vision. You should always have a preferred picture of what you are trying to create. Obviously, your vision should be scaled accordingly.

One way to find the right scale is to think about your time horizon. A frontline leader's vision is often measured in a single shift or day: "What are we trying to accomplish *today?*" A team leader may have a vision for the month while a department leader may look out a quarter at a time. A senior leader's timeline will be even longer, making strategic bets in research and development and innovation projects whose payout could be years in the future.

I know I still haven't answered your question: "What if I don't have a vision?" I'm not trying to dodge the question, but I can't do the work for you, and I am not aware of a proven formula. However, I have included some questions that may be helpful. Your vision for yourself, your team, your organization, or your cause is likely embedded in the answers to these questions.

- What do you want to be true in the future that's not true today?
- What have others done in similar circumstances that might inform your vision?
- What could you pursue that would create new competitive advantage?
- What are we uniquely positioned to do that would enhance our value to customers?
- If time and money were not a factor, how would you describe your perfect life, team, or organization in a decade?
- If you hired a consultant to help you with this, what do you think she would suggest you do next?
- What in your past gives you clues as to what would be advantageous for your future?
- What trends are emerging that could impact your team/organization?
- If you could eliminate all fear of failure, what would you attempt over the next decade?
- How would you describe the future of your life/team/organization or cause in such a way as to generate new levels of passion and excitement in you and those you lead?
- What would have to be true in the future for you to have literally changed the world ten years from now?

I hope these questions don't overwhelm you—that isn't the intent. Crafting a vision is a very personal process most often requiring time, reflection, probing, testing, and more reflection.

Give yourself grace in the process. You are literally trying to see the unseen. Only then, *after* you see it, will you likely have the courage and the opportunity to Create Change.

CAST THE VISION

If you have the most compelling vision in the world and cannot communicate it effectively, it is of little value. Over the years, I have been a bit surprised at the enormity of this challenge. One organization told me that how to communicate vision more effectively was the number one request from their thousands of leaders from around the world. Here are some of my favorite ideas on how to share your vision more effectively.

Say It to Your Inner Circle First

Regardless of whether your vision is big or small, you will need your leaders on board if you hope to turn it into reality. Unfortunately, I see too many leaders skip this step. The consequence: When frontline employees have questions about the vision, who do they turn to? *Their* leader, not the senior leader. If he or she says, "I don't know any more than you do," the entire effort is compromised.

Start with your team and cascade the vision; answer their questions and secure buy-in along the way. You may even want your leaders to help craft the communications and deployment plan for the rest of the team/organization. To skip this step or do it poorly is like fumbling the ball on the one-yard line. The work from the previous ninety-nine yards will be lost.

Say It Often

This is so basic I wouldn't mention it unless it was an almost universal problem. The best leaders talk about the vision *all the time*. Some of the leaders I admire say it in virtually every setting. They say it in emails, and they say it in casual conversations. One global leader I know challenged me to never end any meeting without reminding people of the vision. Jack Welch, the famed CEO of General Electric, said that while attempting to become number one or number two in every market where they competed, he said those words so often he almost gagged on them as they came out of his mouth.[2]

Say It Succinctly

Can you summarize the vision in a word, phrase, or short statement? I was challenged early in my career: if you can't print it on a T-shirt, you don't have it yet. You can always elaborate on the vision: you can give lengthy talks on it, write essays, and produce videos and Power-Point presentations illuminating every detail. But can you state it succinctly? Can you make it memorable—even sticky? For the vision to come to life, it needs to become part of the fabric and daily conversation of an organization and an active filter for decision-making. None of this will happen if the vision is not stated in as few words as possible.

Say It with Passion

If the leader(s) are not passionate about the vision, don't expect the rest of the organization to care much either. Passion is contagious, and so is indifference. People always watch the leader. They are looking for clues: they want to know if you are trustworthy and what's important. Communicating vision unenthusiastically answers both these questions and undermines your effort to lead.

If you say the vision is important and they don't believe you, you will lose trust. If you are not excited about the vision, they will mirror your response. Well, that's not quite accurate—they will fall somewhere just short of your passion. If you want to know the temperature in an organization, stick the thermometer in the leader's mouth—the rest of the people will be a few degrees below the leader.

Say It Strategically

I mentioned the importance of starting with your inner circle; this act alone is a strategic one. Don't stop there. Think about various audiences within your organization—how does the vision need to be personalized and communicated to each one? Think about every stakeholder group, inside and outside the organization. Give special attention to who communicates the message, how they do it, and how often it needs to be repeated and reinforced. I recommend you create a thoughtful, proactive, and multifaceted ongoing communications plan with clear accountability assigned. Your success in accomplishing the vision hinges on several factors—effective communication is on that short list.

Say It with Different Learning Styles in Mind

You may be familiar with Howard Gardner's work at Harvard on multiple intelligences. His work can be earth-shattering for leaders and organizations who wish to reach a broad and diverse group of people. Here's the essence of his findings: different people receive, process, evaluate, and internalize information differently. If Gardner had stopped there, this would not be very helpful. However, he went on to identify different learning modalities—our multiple intelligences. In his book *Frames of Mind*, Gardner[3] outlined seven intelligences:

- Linguistic
- Logical-mathematical
- Spatial
- Bodily-kinesthetic
- Musical
- Interpersonal
- Intrapersonal

Since his original findings were published in 1983, Howard has expanded his list to include the naturalist intelligence (think Charles Darwin or Jane Goodall), but the concept is the same—different people embody different types of "smart." The implication for us as leaders and communicators: we need to convey the vision in ways it will resonate with our diverse audience, not just focus on our preferred method.

If you want to learn more, Thomas Armstrong wrote a very approachable translation of Gardner's academic work called *Seven Kinds of Smart.*[4]

Here is a high-level summary of a project I led for a nonprofit attempting to raise money for a new building using the seven kinds of smart as a strategic communications framework.

- **Art Smart**. These people are most likely to get the vision through a visual depiction. Application: We commissioned a large color rendering of the proposed building.

- **Word Smart**. Words, spoken or written, connect best with these folks. Application: We created a newsletter to track the progress of the campaign, along with a brochure outlining all the details.

- **Math Smart**. What are the facts? The statistics? The numbers? That's the primary language of these people. Application: The team published the stats. We told people about the square footage of the proposed building and the car count driving by the new location.

- **Body Smart.** These people want to physically interact with the vision. Application: The team organized tours of the new property. Not everyone showed up—but the body smart people did!

- **People Smart.** Conversation helps these people understand concepts and ideas. Application: Small group meetings were organized so people could hear the vision and ask questions of senior leaders.

- **Self Smart.** Personal reflection is the preferred method to gain understanding for this group. Application: The team created a self-study guide allowing those who wanted to work through the vision on their own to do so.

- **Music Smart.** For these people, music is their primary mode for connecting with and internalizing information. Application: The team selected a theme song for the campaign. We gave all potential donors a CD of the song so those who wanted to could listen and internalize the vision.

You and I need to get this vision thing right. I framed the chapters that support each Smart Choice as best practices—I'll confess, this chapter isn't labeled correctly—vision is not a best practice, it is essential if you really want to Create Change and scale your impact.

A leader has many tools and resources at his or her disposal to Create Change—staff, research, time, consultants, team building, downsizing, outsourcing, Lean, Six Sigma, money, artificial intelligence, technology, automation, and more. However, to what end?

People are not generally energized for long because of a new *how*. Only a compelling *why* will animate and call forth the needed creativity, engagement, and excellence. Leaders must see it clearly and say it plainly and often, to transport people to a better tomorrow—first in their minds, then their hearts. Then, and only then, with a lot of hard work, can you make the vision a reality.

BE SMART!

Although there are several questions in the previous chapters intended to help you clarify your vision, I suggest you take this one and give it a try.

What do you want to be true in a decade that is not true today?

Answer this question *twice*—once as it relates to your leadership, and second, personally. Your answer may not represent your fully orbed vision, but it should provide solid clues. You will not create what you cannot articulate.

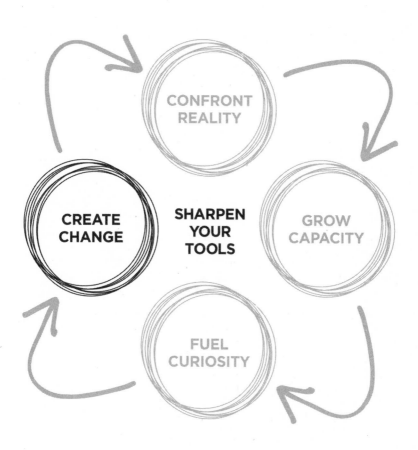

SHARPEN YOUR TOOLS

"All things are difficult before they are easy."
Thomas Fuller

On June 20, 1997, Captain Michael Abrashoff reported to the USS *Benfold*, an 8,600-ton guided-missile destroyer in the US Navy's Pacific Fleet. When the new skipper arrived for the transfer of command ceremony, he was struck by the deportment of the crew. When the former captain was piped ashore, the cheers were not of appreciation or well wishes; they were jeers of celebration for his departure. Mike recalls his embarrassment for the departing leader and couldn't help but wonder what his future transfer of power would be like. All he knew was he didn't want his story to end like the previous captain.

As Abrashoff took command, the ship was a wreck—not a physical shipwreck, but it was in deep trouble. The performance was low; Mike told me the *Benfold* was rated the worst ship in the fleet. The crew was disengaged and disheartened, and the reenlistment rate of the sailors was 28 percent compared to about a 75 percent rate for the rest of the navy.

For months, the new captain worked diligently to listen to his crew. He wanted to help them achieve their goals. He also wanted them to take ownership of the ship. One of many tactics he employed was a one-on-one meeting with each sailor—all 310 of them. These listening sessions proved pivotal in the change effort.

Fast-forward twenty months, and the ship was recognized as the most combat-ready ship in the fleet. Its crew had 100 percent reenrollment, and the ship was operating on only 75 percent of its budget. Higher engagement, the highest retention possible, lower costs, and outstanding performance—every leader's dream!

What did Captain Abrashoff do to lead this impressive change effort? To get all the details, you will want to read his book *It's Your Ship*,[1] but to summarize, he did what all effective leaders do. He used the tools of the trade—the trade of leadership.

Along the way, Mike also put the needs of his crew above his own preferences and bias. I believe Mike would tell you long-term systemic change is impossible unless the leader is willing to set their own ego aside. Remember: he titled his first book *It's Your Ship*.

Unfortunately, most large-scale change efforts do not have happy endings like the USS *Benfold*. On the contrary, according to numerous studies, the majority fail. A study published in the *Harvard Business Review* found a whopping 75 percent of change efforts did *not* achieve their stated objectives or were abandoned altogether.[2] A Gallup study reached an eerily similar conclusion, citing a failure rate of 70 percent.[3] I don't want to move past these factoids too quickly. Let's put them in context.

A leader's primary role is to create positive change—to help people and organizations move from here to there—there being a preferred future. If the majority of our efforts fail, what type of grade do these leaders deserve? To me, this is one of the more sobering realities and challenges leaders face. Despite all our good intentions and grand visions, can we actually help our people and our organizations create a better tomorrow? Can we Create Change? This is the ultimate test of leadership.

Let's briefly revisit the case I've already tried to make. One of the primary obstacles standing defiantly between us and our visons is the quicksand many leaders are swimming in every day. We have to get out if we are going to do our jobs. Leaders mired in distractions and encumbrances of any sort cannot effectively and efficiently Create Change. How could they? They are just trying to survive.

The Smart Choices are the stepping-stones out of the quicksand and can pave the way to higher ground. However, I'll say it again—each choice must be lived out. It must be activated. That is what the best practice chapters are intended to do, none more so than this chapter.

If a leader declares, "I choose to Create Change," this is admirable. Honestly, it is even expected if you are in fact attempting to lead. Without informed and thoughtful action, however, this statement is nothing more than lip service. Our actions ultimately validate our resolve.

CHANGE IS HARD

Change is extremely difficult to orchestrate. If positive change was easy to deliver, the world would have an overabundant supply of leaders. It doesn't. To Create Change in service of a better tomorrow is our calling and our contribution. We help make people, organizations, and the world better by the change efforts we lead.

As a leader, with Creating Change squarely at the heart of your job description, you have probably given some thought to the following questions: Why is change so hard? What can I do to make it easier?

Have you ever needed to do something around the house and realized you didn't have the right tool? It could be as simple as removing a single, very tiny screw to unlock the battery compartment on a child's toy, but if you don't have the right screwdriver, that little plastic door might as well be welded shut.

Sometimes the project may be a little more challenging. Most recently, I was attempting to change a light bulb over a stairwell. After trying to figure out how to stabilize my stepladder while precariously perched over the steps, I decided it wouldn't work. After a trip to the local home improvement store, I returned with an extension ladder engineered with adjustable legs so it would easily work on stairs—exactly what it was designed to do. What seemed impossible (and dangerous) an hour earlier became really simple. Having the right tool matters.

As a leader, you face a multitude of problems—sometimes on a daily basis. In most cases, you'll need three things: your expertise, the right tools, and the will to address the problem. If I had been comfortable living with a dark stairwell, no intervention or tool would have been required.

You already have a toolbox full of methods, strategies, tactics, and tools at your disposal. And to be clear, I don't have any new tools to give you today. What I will do is challenge you to dust off some tools and practices and give them another try.

Tools are interesting devices—they are full of latent possibility waiting to be directed and their potentials released, but tools rarely work by themselves. You must provide the intention, direction, and the human touch to release their power.

TOOLS OF CHANGE

What follows is a partial list of tools every leader *already* has in his or her bag. The trick is twofold:

1. Do we know *how* to use them?
2. Do we know *when* to use them?

The complete answers to these questions are beyond the scope of this book. If you are unfamiliar with any of these, or just haven't used them recently, perhaps you can look for an opportunity to put them to work on your next challenge. You may even want to ask a mentor or colleague to help you sharpen your skills. The magic in a tool always lives in the craftsman who directs it.

Passion

I know we have already devoted a full chapter to vision, but I cannot talk about the tools of change without starting here. As I reflected on which facet of vision is most critical, I was struck by the passion the leader needs to bring to the conversation. As John Maxwell and others have said for decades, "Everything rises and falls on leadership." This is true at many levels but when it comes to change, what you are passionate about will color everything you do. Your passion will drive how you use your time, influence your communications, what you recognize, what you tolerate, and what you address. It will even filter down to the reports you read and the meetings you attend.

If you want to Create Change and use vision to ignite the change in your organization, you will need to check your passion—it is the kindling to start the fires of change. If the vision doesn't fire you up, you can forget anyone else investing their heart and soul in helping you keep the fires burning.

The Gift of Accountability

This is a tool that probably doesn't get the attention or respect it deserves. I have spent time over the years trying to figure out why so many leaders miss the power of this simple idea. I think accountability needs a public relations campaign and perhaps a renowned branding agency to give it a new image. I believe accountability is a good thing, not a bad thing. Here's a quick defense of this counter-cultural view.

I believe most people want to be successful in life and work. To be successful, you have to do the things you need to do and the things you say you will do. However, we all know stuff happens and we can easily get off track. That is where accountability comes in. When we give someone the gift of accountability, we are helping them be successful.

I was once asked which part of a kite is most critical for sustained flight. I didn't know but began to name the parts of a kite: the tail, the sail, the sticks or structure. I quickly ran out of options. I thought, *A kite doesn't have that many parts.*

I was told I had it all wrong—the thing that allows a kite to soar is the string. Without the tension of being tethered to someone on the ground (accountability), it will quickly crash, if it even gets off the ground in the first place.

One more thought on accountability: it comes in all shapes and sizes—leader to team, peer to peer, process or system accountability, outcome or goal accountability, a coach, mentor, accountability partner, and self-accountability, to name a few. In virtually every circumstance, having people and processes in place to help you do what you want and need to do is a good thing.

If you want to take some baby steps, try ending every meeting with a review of the action items—a list of who is going to do what by when. Then, at your next meeting, review the previous action items to check status, see if anyone needs assistance, and to give the gift of accountability. I have witnessed firsthand this simple practice revolutionize multimillion-dollar organizations. One leader confided in me, "Before, we were really good at talking about things—now we actually do them." Now that's a gift that keeps on giving!

Goals and Measurement

As a reminder, I shared some of the benefits of goals in the chapter entitled "Review Your Crew" in the context of building a winning team. All of those benefits are also applicable on a larger organizational scale—goals unify people, clarify priorities, drive strategies, affect resource allocation, impact structure, improve performance, create energy and urgency. Goals also help people keep score.

When thinking about a specific change effort, what should be included on your scorecard? Obviously, the answer will depend on what you are trying to accomplish. However, I have three suggestions.

- Think in terms of a family of metrics versus a single one. If you can identify a single indicator, fantastic, but rarely are things so simple.
- Keep the number of metrics limited. I don't think there is a magic number, but the right answer is closer to five than ten. If you believe tracking other metrics would be helpful, track away—as supporting data.
- Hold your scorecard loosely—it is a tool. Ultimately, the objective isn't to keep score, it is to successfully Create Change and a better tomorrow. If the scorecard needs to change, change it.

I wrote about the visceral feeling people have when keeping score and the equally powerful emotions associated with not keeping score in my book *Win Every Day*. Here's a quick recap of the story I told there.

During a recent training session, we took 150 leaders bowling. But there was a twist: we covered up the pins. They were instructed to bowl. When they protested, we reminded them their job was to roll the ball.

After just a few minutes, their energy, enthusiasm, and engagement were at rock bottom. They had turned their attention to their phones, the video games in the bowling alley, and the occasional, unhelpful jab at a fellow bowler. Then, after about forty-five minutes, we uncovered the pins—and everything changed. Their energy was back, the fun returned to a familiar game, they were cheering for each other, with some occasional smack talk, and they began to keep score.

At the end of the second round, another forty-five minutes, we stopped the action and asked the group to consider how they felt during the first round.

"It sucked," volunteered one young man.

"I just didn't care," said another. Others agreed. After hearing several stories of apathy and lack of purpose, we then asked about the second round. Their responses were, as you would expect, totally different. They mentioned fun, engaging, encouraging, and more.

To close the evening, I asked the group one final question: "How was round one (where you couldn't see the pins) any different than the experience of the men and women in your organization who have never 'seen the pins' and do not know the score?"

People love to keep score. If you help them, they will help you Create Change.

Values

Values in a corporate setting are interesting. I can confidently argue they may be the least-often-used, most-neglected tools in your leadership toolbox. Because I am a huge fan of values as a tool of change and have used them with some success throughout my career, I am puzzled by leaders who fail to wield them frequently.

Here's my two-cents worth on values. Most people in an organization want to do a good job. I'll take that a step further: most people also want to please their leader. This is a form of career preservation and enlightened self-interest. Now, consider what values are: the beliefs the organization would like to see drive individual and collective behavior.

If I am an employee who wants to make good in my career, I'm keenly interested in knowing the behaviors (values) the organization values. This alignment alone can create positive movement. Add to this the impact clear and stated values can have on who you recruit, select, recognize, and reward, and you will find values, properly leveraged, are one of the most efficient and effective tools you have at your disposal to create positive change.

Planning

Planning is another tool many leaders undervalue. However, the ability to create a solid, actionable, effective plan is gold to leaders who want to productively Create Change. If you embrace your role as the architect of the future, planning is the process by which you create the blueprints.

When my wife and I met with a builder to discuss the prospects of building our first house, we were excited. I remember giving him my plan for our new house. In reality, it was nothing more than a hand-drawn floor plan. However, I was proud of it. I had drawn it to scale.

A few weeks later, we met with the builder again, and he pulled out a *full* set of blueprints. The sketch we had provided him was woefully inadequate to actually build a house. It was a fair representation of the concept, but included nothing about the foundation, the plumbing, the electrical, the roof, the front, back, and side elevations, the topographical map showing the placement of the house, or the detailed drawings needed for trim work.

As leaders, we may be able to draw a simple diagram on the back of a napkin representing our vision. There are countless such stories from the start-ups in Silicon Valley alone. However, a vision, regardless of how clear and compelling it is, must have credible plans created to ensure it will actually work as designed once it is built.

My encouragement to leaders is simple: invest adequate time in planning. I have rarely met a leader who can honestly say they overinvest in this most critical behavior. This may seem counterintuitive. I have encountered too many leaders who consider planning beneath them. Their attitude and sometimes their sentiment is *"Shouldn't we be doing real work?"*

As leaders, our job is to build a team or organization capable of creating a better tomorrow. Before you release your organization to begin the process, wouldn't you want them to have all the pages of the blueprints?

Communication

As I look back on my career, and the thousands of organizations I have observed, I have no doubt ongoing communication is the *most important* tool you have to Create Change. Unfortunately, many leaders don't agree with me. However, I am not alone in my call for more thoughtful, strategic, ongoing communications to animate change.

John Kotter, the former professor at Harvard Business School and the author of the book *Leading Change,* also sees an opportunity in this area. In an article he wrote for the *Harvard Business Review,*[4] Kotter says after studying one hundred corporate change efforts, he estimated they were *under-communicating by a factor of ten!*

Leaders are often too busy moving on to the next new thing to successfully implement the last new thing. Energy is needed to sustain the long march required for most change efforts. This energy can find its source in the consistent, aligned messages of the change effort.

Why is communication so critical in times of change? Most people do not like change or are threatened by it, and many may be uncertain regarding how the changes proposed will impact them personally. In the absence of a story, people will make one up. Why not be the one authoring the story?

Be sure key messages are simple, repeatable, consistent, and persistent. Don't be too quick to move on to the next big idea. If you miss this, you will guarantee the last big idea will never come to fruition.

Recognition

The last of the tools we will review here is a powerhouse. If you want to create new behaviors, recognize the women and men who demonstrate the new behaviors. The flip side is true as well. If you recognize, celebrate, and acknowledge people who do not align with the new vision and demonstrate the desired behaviors, you will sabotage your own change effort. Just like many of the tools we have just reviewed, they come in all shapes and sizes. Recognition is not a one-size-fits-all proposition.

If you want to test me on this, try an experiment. Meet with five members of your organization for a brief one-on-one call or meeting. I suggest you select a diverse group for this activity—younger, older, new to the company, a veteran, different levels and jobs within your team. Once you have your group set, ask each person one question: Will you please tell me about the best personal recognition you have ever received?

I have done this with scores of my team members over the years, and I want to predict what you are going to hear. They are all going to share several different types of recognition. Some will like public recognition, preferably in front of their peers. Others will want a trophy or plaque to display. Still others are going to reflect on a handwritten note from a supervisor, and don't be surprised if someone says their best recognition was a day off. The more you do this, the more diverse answers you will hear.

What's the point of this experiment? To sensitize you to the uniqueness and individuality of your team members and to remind you to listen and pay attention. Recognition *is* powerful if done thoughtfully and individualized as much as possible.

———

So where does all of this leave us? We have access to the tools. They are not costly or hard to find, but they do require discipline, intentionality, and practice to master them. The work required to Create Change is challenging—but it is our work.

I love the way the American motivational writer William Ward described differing responses to the wind: "The pessimist complains about the wind; the optimist expects it to change; the realist adjusts the sails."

I believe leaders should be realists. If we are going to make the Smart Choice to Create Change, we had better be in the business of adjusting the sails, and to do that well, we'll need some tools.

TROUBLESHOOTING GUIDE

This is my opportunity to remind you: Creating Change is much easier when you employ the tools we just reviewed. However, sometimes the solution will *not* be found in the tool itself. If you are finding it exceedingly difficult to see any progress on your journey (and you've made the first three Smart Choices), ask yourself if you're facing some of these common issues.

Is the Vision Clear?

When you cannot figure out what is wrong with your TV or some other electronic device, have you ever looked at the troubleshooting guide? If you do, I can almost guarantee you the first item is going to be *Ensure the device is plugged in.*

If you are having trouble getting your change effort moving, check the power source—the vision. The vision should provide a ready source of energy for you and the organization. One of my mentors was fond of saying, "If there is mist in the pulpit, there will be fog in the pews." Translated, the vision will never be clearer among your people than it is in your heart and mind. Vision is one of your most powerful tools if it is clear and compelling. You will find it extremely difficult to rally people to a future you cannot articulate clearly.

Now, this isn't to suggest every detail of the future is knowable—obviously it is not. However, the vision needs enough clarity and specificity to engage support. Vague, ambiguous, ill-defined vision is no vision at all. Because we dealt with this subject in depth in the previous chapter, I'll land with this: Without vison, there is no energy source—there is no leadership.

Is Your Organization Suffering from ADHD?

For those who may not know, ADHD stands for attention-deficit/hyperactivity disorder—a life-altering condition affecting millions of people around the world. I don't use this term lightly or flippantly. As I attempted to name the condition I see afflicting organizations large and small around the world, however, this was the perfect analogy. Here is a partial list of common symptoms of ADHD in humans:

- Inattention
- Impulsivity
- Hyperactivity
- Lacks attention to detail
- Poor listening skills
- Avoids activities requiring full engagement
- Easily distracted
- Driven, as if addicted to activity
- Talks a lot

These are the *same issues* many organizations face when attempting to make a significant change. Unfortunately, the behaviors and tendencies listed are at war with productive, sustainable change. The good news: ADHD is treatable, in humans and organizations. For your purposes, a healthy dose of vision, measurement, and accountability will go a long way toward combating this affliction.

Is There Sufficient Urgency to Create the Change You Desire?

Because of the inherent difficulty in significant change, in virtually every situation, urgency will be required. This urgency must begin with the leader, but it cannot stop there. Urgency must cascade down and throughout the organization. If this urgency fails to make its way all the way to the front lines, sustained change is unlikely. Lack of urgency can quickly become a lack of action; a lack of action creates a stronghold for the status quo. The result: another failed change effort.

Is There Alignment?

The larger the organization, the more likely you are to find alignment issues. However, don't dismiss this as an issue for large, multinational organizations alone. If a team of five people is not aligned on a significant change effort, the odds of success plummet.

I am reminded of how many times over the years I have been told I needed to purchase new tires—not because I had a nail in the tire, but because my car had been out of alignment. Am I the only one this has happened to? I think not. It's not that I don't care about keeping my car aligned; I'm just too busy going places. Most organizations want alignment; they just do not give enough attention to it.

Communication is the primary antidote for this issue—strategic, aligned, consistent, and frequent messages delivered by multiple voices in multiple channels. The gift of accountability also never hurts when attempting to maintain alignment.

Are Your Expectations Realistic?

I am referring to both the scope of what you are trying to accomplish and the speed at which you are trying to move. Let's face it: sometimes our change efforts fail because we attempt to do too much too fast. I'm always a fan of aiming high. However, as leaders, we have to be careful. If our vision is to be the best in the world at something, that's fine, but depending on where you are today, it may take longer than one annual planning cycle to get there.

Another tendency that fits here is underresourced plans and aspirations. Perhaps the goal is reasonable, but the resources, most commonly money and people, are insufficient, Leaders also must be mindful of the amount of change an organization can metabolize. As Henry Cloud says, "Too much, too fast, and the organization will cast it off."

I saw the flip side of this a few years ago in a multibillion-dollar organization. Senior leaders had come up with a compelling, potentially game-changing vision. Thankfully, they went to the people who would have to do the work and asked about the resources required to turn their intention into reality. The teams responded with a plan to accomplish the vision. The organization could not fund the vision, at least not at the pace they first desired. To their credit, leadership right sized the change effort based on the resources available.

―――――

I realize after working through the list above, you might summarize all of these issues under a single heading: lack of leadership. While this may be true, it isn't constructive. Hopefully, by naming these various potential problems and barriers, you can more likely avoid them in the future. However, avoidance is never enough to create the future we see. Avoiding junk food is good for your body but no substitute for exercise. To invest our days merely trying to avoid potential impediments would be like a team *only* playing defense— don't get me wrong, defense matters, but ultimately, your team has to score if you are going to win.

The ability to Create Change is at the heart of your job description. Defense alone will not get you there. If you are aware of these typical failure points, while proactively and strategically using the tools of change, not only will you be on offense, you will successfully Create Change and build a better tomorrow!

BE SMART!

Go back and look at the troubleshooting section of this chapter. Identify any of these causes which may have hampered your past change efforts. Begin creating a plan to eliminate, or at least mitigate, this issue from your next change effort.

BE SMART!

"Harry . . . yer a wizard."
Hagrid

A cross the eight Harry Potter movies, there were many pivotal moments. But the one that totally changed the course of the entire storyline came when Harry received his life-altering visit from Hagrid on the evening of his eleventh birthday.

It was time for Harry to go to Hogwarts and learn how to develop his skills as a wizard. There was only one issue—Harry didn't know he was a wizard. Then, with a calmness that masked the significance of the pronouncement, Hagrid, looking down at the boy, said, "Harry . . . yer a wizard."

Can you imagine what was going through young Harry Potter's mind the moment he learned of his magical power? It seems only fitting at the end of this book to bring you the same message:

Yer a wizard too!

You have amazing power, and like Harry, it will take some work to make those powers productive, but you're on your way. The choices you've explored throughout this book are a wonderful next step on your leadership journey—and you don't have to travel to Hogwarts to practice your newfound powers. To leverage your special gift, you will have to make the choice to do so—four of them, specifically.

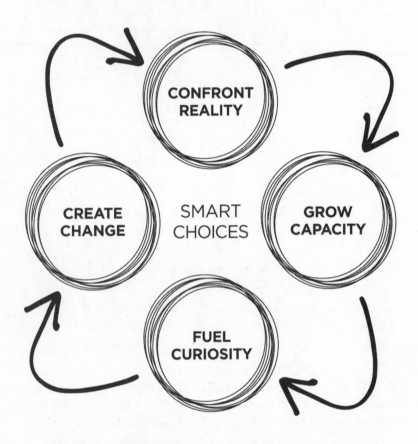

Confront Reality to stay grounded in truth and lead from a position of strength.

Grow Capacity to meet the demands of the moment and the challenges of the future.

Fuel Curiosity to maintain relevance and vitality in a changing world.

Create Change today to ensure a better tomorrow.

Will you make these four simple, life-giving choices? *Your* vision hangs in the balance—your influence, your impact, and your legacy as well. I believe you can do it. Armed with these choices, I think progress is imminent and your success inevitable.

Although I cannot predict your level of success or the depth of your impact on the world, I can boldly and confidently tell you one thing: you will never regret making these choices.

More than forty years into my leadership journey, I'm more thankful than ever that you and I have the opportunity to choose. I also realize how difficult it is to consistently make the right choice. I could write another book on my poor choices, but you wouldn't want to read that one. But when we mess up, we can stand back up and make our next, better choice.

The most exciting part of your story has yet to be written. When you choose wisely, those you lead and the organization you serve will be the beneficiaries. I'm thankful our success as leaders will ultimately be determined by our choices. No more swimming in quicksand.

I look forward to seeing you leading from higher ground!

ACKNOWLEDGMENTS

As a guy who has written and spoken a lot of words in my life, I am never more at a loss for the *right* words than when I try to convey my appreciation for the women and men who make something like this book possible. I am so thankful for the people who helped bring these ideas to life.

For those who have read any of my previous work, you know this was a fundamentally different approach than our previous attempts to serve leaders. Not only were we trying to articulate what the best leaders do (so the rest of us could emulate them) but we were also trying to incorporate the leading thinking of others as well. Therefore, I'm confident we did more pure research on this work than any of our other projects—thousands of hours spanning several years.

We certainly did the always-productive traditional interviews, but we also did extensive work to discern the emerging and timeless truths that would ultimately become the Smart Choices. Add to this the scores, if not hundreds, of case studies and best practices we discovered along the way, and you can begin to appreciate the mountain of information we compiled. Although many of those findings informed our conclusions, they are not directly reflected in the final manuscript. Just last week, I cut ten thousand words from the final draft!

Why am I telling you all of this? To help you grasp the enormity of the task the women and men I am about to recognize did to bring you these simple Smart Choices and their accompanying best practices. As I have always believed, on virtually every issue, there is simplicity on the other side of complexity. On this project, the team went to the dark and twisted heart of complexity and emerged with timeless truth.

The Core Team: Kate Elkin, Mausum Shah, Ashlee Davidhizar, Mike Fleming, Michael Barry, Michelle Jia, Yuri Zaitsev, Jillian Broaddus, Jessica Hampton, and Randy Gravitt. Your spirit of curiosity was evident from the day we began this work. You pushed my thinking beyond where I had been previously and then pushed again. You wanted both truth and simplicity. After pursuing this topic personally for more than forty years, you helped me grow during this process. Not only will our readers benefit from your work, I will too. You were a dream team. Thank you.

The Leaders: Thanks to the hard work of the team, we were able to talk with the most diverse group of leaders we have ever assembled. We interviewed CEOs, a music director, a military leader, entrepreneurs, academics, a few leadership coaches and consultants, nonprofit leaders, a psychologist, several company founders, financial executives, a leader from a professional sports league, packaged-goods leaders, accounting services leaders, and a kung fu grandmaster. Many of these women and men work in global businesses. The pages of this book drip with their distilled wisdom. Here are some of the leaders we interviewed:

Deborah Ancona, Shane Benson, James Blachly, Dan Christman, Roger Clarke, Luke Cook, Caroline Dudley, Bill Dunphy, Michael Edmonds, Bob Garrett, Kathy Giusti, Quart Graves, Kevin Harrison, Jack Lannom, Dr. Hal M. Lewis, Lauren McGuire, Geetha Murali, Kathleen Price, Jim Quigley, Prakash Raman, Shamal Ranasinghe, Cliff Robinson, Dean Sandbo, Todd Sandel, D. Sangeeta, Eileen Serra, Paul Sierleja, Doug Smith, Amy Jen Su, David

Sykora, Elizabeth Talerman, Michael Walkup, Aaron Williams, Brad Williams, and Kevin Williams.

The Reviewers: In addition to the core team, I asked a few others to read an early draft of this work. I called it "Draft Zero." They helped clarify and improve what you just read. Thanks to Janice Rutledge, Justin Miller, Donna Miller, Dr. Tim Miller, Dean Sandbo, Edgar Brush, Zach Clark, Robert Throckmorton, Charmain Bather, Randy Cochran, and Brittany Miller.

The Publishing Team: Finally, thanks to: Alex Field, Matt Holt, Katie Dickman, Brigid Pearson, Mallory Hyde, Jay Kilburn, and the leadership at BenBella. Thanks for believing we can change the world by serving leaders.

ADDITIONAL RESOURCES

I trust you found value in what you've just read. In the Smart Choices, some of you have discovered your next step to scale your impact. Congratulations! For others, your next learning objective is to revisit some of the fundamental skills of leadership or to continue fortifying your leadership character.

Regardless of what's next for you, my team and I have created many other resources to assist you. We have additional books, field guides, assessments, videos, and more to help you build your own High Performance Organization (HPO). Also, although I do very few speaking engagements, I do have men and women I can highly recommend to speak to your organization on the content of this book or any of the HPO material. These are seasoned and dynamic communicators who have spoken to tens of thousands of people. I can also recommend trainers and coaches if you believe this would serve you and your organization. You can learn more about all of this at MarkMillerLeadership.com.

NOTES

SWIMMING IN QUICKSAND

1. Michael E. Porter and Nitin Nohria, *How CEOs Manage Their Time* (Harvard Business Publishing, 2018).
2. John Brandon, "These Updated Stats about How Often You Use Your Phone Will Humble You," Inc.com, November 19, 2019.
3. Teodora Dobrilova, "35+ Must-Know SMS Marketing Statistics in 2021," TechJury.net, June 15, 2021.
4. Joseph Johnson, "Number of Sent & Received E-mails per Day Worldwide from 2017 to 2025," Statista.com, April 7, 2021.
5. H. Tankovska, "Number of Social Network Users Worldwide from 2017 to 2025," Statista.com, January 28, 2021.
6. "Total Audience Report Q1 2019," Nielsen Company.
7. "Instagram by the Numbers," Omnicoreagency.com, August 1, 2021.
8. Danny Donchev, "37 Mind Blowing YouTube Facts, Figures and Statistics—2021," Fortunelords.com, May 26, 2021.
9. Nicholas Carr, *The Shallows* (W. W. Norton, June 7, 2010).
10. Brigid Schulte, "Work Interruptions Can Cost You 6 Hours a Day," *Washington Post*, June 1, 2015.
11. Deyan G., "How Many Websites Are There in 2021?" TechJury .net, March 16, 2021.

12. "How Many Apps Are There in the World," DotNek.com, February 13, 2021.

13. Howard Slutsken, "Four Million Parts, 30 Countries," CNN.com, December 28, 2018.

14. UNESCO Institute of Statistics.

15. Keira Wingate, *"The Worst Cereal You Should Never Eat,"* eatthis .com, December 2020.

16. "Changing Channels: Americans View Just 17 Channels Despite Record Number to Choose From," Nielsen Insights, May 6, 2014.

YOUR REAL SUPERPOWER

1. Simon Sinek, "How Great Leaders Inspire Action," TEDx Puget Sound, September 2009.

2. Baba Shiv, "How to Make Better Decisions," Stanford Business School, January 2013.

3. Shai Danziger, Jonathan Leva, and Liora Avnaim-Pesso, "External Factors in Judicial Decisions," *Proceedings of the National Academy of Sciences of the United States of America (PNAS)*, April 26, 2011.

4. Saul McLeod, "Solomon Asch: Conformity Experiment," *Simply Psychology*, December 28, 2018.

CONFRONT REALITY

1. J. P. Donlon, "Medtronic CEO Bill George Still Searching for Authenticity," ChiefExecutive.net, October 13, 2009.

2. Andrew Martins, "Study Finds Mentors Are Important," *Business News Daily*, March 30, 2019.

3. Napoleon Hill, *Think and Grow Rich*, March 1937.

CHECK THE MIRROR

1. Antonio Neves, "What One CEO Did When 45 of Her Employees Quit, *Inc.*, October 16, 2017.
2. Peter Drucker, *The Effective Executive* (New York: Harper & Row, 1967).
3. Victor Lipman, "Do Higher-Level Leaders Have Lower Self-Awareness?" *Forbes*, April 2018.
4. "Engagement," Gallup, 2020.
5. Julian Watkins, *The 100 Greatest Advertisements: 1852–1958* (Dover Publications, February 15, 2012).

REVIEW YOUR CREW

1. "100 Greatest Moments in Sports History," *Sports Illustrated*, March 2016.
2. Rob Cross, Reb Rebele, and Adam Grant, "Collaborative Overload," *Harvard Business Review*—January–February 2016.
3. 2019 Deloitte Global Human Capital Trends.

GROW CAPACITY

1. "Ford's Assembly Line Starts Rolling," History.com.
2. Kevin Jackson, "The 5 Fastest Supercomputers in the World," *Science Node*, June 2020.
3. *Do Your Job: Bill Belichick & the 2014 Patriots*, NFL Films.
4. Peter Drucker, *The Effective Executive* (New York: Harper & Row, 1967).
5. Howard Gardner, *Leading Minds* (Basic Books, 2011).
6. T. D. Jakes, *Leadership Summit*, 2017.

STOP AND THINK

1. Michael E. Porter and Nitin Nohria, "How CEOs Manage Time," *Harvard Business Review*, July–August 2018.
2. Ronald Heifetz, *Leadership without Easy Answers* (Harvard University Press, 1998).
3. George Santayana, *The Life of Reason*, 1905.

EXPAND YOUR ENERGY

1. Jeff Pfeffer and Bob Sutton, *The Knowing-Doing Gap* (Harvard Business School Publishing, January 15, 2000).
2. "Too Tired to Function Safely at Work," National Safety Council, July 2017.
3. Steve Tappin and Andrew Cave, *The Secrets of CEOs*, 2008.
4. Jeffrey M. Jones, "In U.S., 40% Get Less Than Recommended Amount of Sleep," *Gallup*, December 19, 2013.
5. The Great British Sleep Survey, 2012.
6. *Research on Drowsy Driving*, National Highway Traffic Safety Administration, 2009.
7. Jack Linshi, "The Most Well-Rested and Sleep-Deprived Cities in the World," *Time*, August 18, 2014.
8. Marco Hafmer, Martin Stepanek, Jirka Taylor, Wendy M. Troxel, Christian van Stolk, "Why Sleep Matters: Economic Costs," *Rand Health Qtrly*, January 2017.
9. Arianna Huffington, *The Sleep Revolution* (Harmony Books, April 5, 2016).
10. Centers for Disease Control and Prevention website, May 2021.
11. Eric J. Olson, "How Many Hours of Sleep Are Enough for Good Health?" Mayo Clinic website, May 15, 2021.

FUEL CURIOSITY

1. Roger von Oech and George Willett, *A Whack on the Side of the Head* (Warner Books, 1983).
2. Larry Miller, *Barbarians to Bureaucrats* (Fawcett Columbine, 1989).
3. Stephen Dowling, "Napster Turns 20," *BBC*, May 31, 2019.
4. Francesca Gino, "The Business Case for Curiosity," *Harvard Business Review*, September–October 2018.
5. Jim Kwik, *Limitless* (Hay House, 2020).
6. Cindi May, "A Learning Secret: Don't Take Notes with a Laptop," *Scientific American*, June 3, 2014.

ASK, DON'T TELL

1. "Favorite Interview Questions," *Business Insider*, February 2021.

TALK WITH STRANGERS

1. Brian Grazer and Charles Fishman, *A Curious Mind: The Secret to a Bigger Life* (Simon & Schuster, April 7, 2015).

CREATE CHANGE

1. Carol Dweck, *Mindset* (Random House, February 28, 2006).
2. Tchiki Davis, "15 Ways to Build a Growth Mindset," *Psychology Today*, April 11, 2019.
3. "What to Do When It's Your Turn" episode with Seth Godin, *The Unmistakable Creative Podcast*.
4. Geoffrey Canada, Harlem Children's Zone, HCZ.org.

SEE THE UNSEEN

1. William Duggin, *Strategic Intuition* (Columbia Business School Publishing, October 18, 2007).
2. Jack Welch, *Jack: Straight from the Gut* (Business Plus, October 1, 2003).
3. Howard Gardner, *Frames of Mind* (Basic Books, March 29, 2011).
4. Thomas Armstrong, *Seven Kinds of Smart* (Plume, October 1, 1999).

SHARPEN YOUR TOOLS

1. Captain D. Michael Abrashoff, *It's Your Ship: Management Techniques from the Best Damn Ship in the Navy* (Grand Central Publishing, 2007).
2. N. Anand and Jean-Louis Barsoux, "What Everyone Gets Wrong about Change," *Harvard Business Review*, November–December 2017.
3. David Leonard and Claude Coltea, "Most Change Initiatives Fail—But They Don't Have To," *Business Journal*, Gallup News, May 24, 2013.
4. John Kotter, "Leading Change: Why Transformation Efforts Fail," *Harvard Business Review*, May–June 1995.

INDEX

A

Abrashoff, Michael, 216–217
accomplishment, vs. activity, 39
accountability, 4, 63, 93, 220–221
action, proximity to, 109
action items, 221
activity. *See also* busyness; roles
  vs. accomplishment, 39
  addiction to, 94–95
  focus on, 109
  reducing tasks, 92–93, 103
adaptability, 142
ADHD, 228
affirmation, 24
After Action Review (AAR),
  114–115
age, 26
agency, 4, 22, 189. *See also* change;
  growth mindset; locus of
  control
aimlessness, 16–17
alcohol, 130
alignment issues, 229
answers, 138, 140
appearance, vs. performance, 39
Aristotle, 109
Armstrong, Thomas, 211–212

arrogance, 38
Asch, Solomon, 26
Ask, Don't Tell, 156–169. *See also*
  questions
assembly line, 88
assessment, 54. *See also* Confront
  Reality; mirror, checking
assumptions/biases, 23, 25, 46
attention-deficit/hyperactivity
  disorder, 228
avoidance response, 25

B

baby steps, 192, 198
Barbarians to Bureaucrats (Miller),
  140
baseball, 74
behaviors, personal experience
  and, 46
Belichick, Bill, 91
belief bias, 25
beliefs/values, 24, 223–224
  articulating, 24
  choices and, 24
  living, 61–62
  personal experience and, 46
  spiritual practices, 42, 132–133

benchmarking, 181
Benfold, USS, 216–217
biases, 23, 25, 46
Biehl, Bobb, 205
blame, vs. responsibility, 63
Blanchard, Ken, 64, 109
blind spots, 41, 43
Blockbuster, 140
board of directors, personal,
47–49
board relations, 48
Bonaparte, Napoleon, 202–203
brain fog, 121–122
brains, 23, 24–25, 149
brainstorming, 164–165. *See also*
problem-solving
brand loyalty, 2
Branson, Richard, 165
Brooks, Herb, 73
Built to Last (Collins), 156
business. *See* organizations
busyness, 39. *See also* activity
vs. hurry, 102
stepping out of, 109, 110. *see
also* margin
Butterfield, Stewart, 166

C
calendar
cleaning up, 91–93
eliminating activities from,
103
focus days on, 113
Canada, Geoffrey, 198–199
capacity, 89, 93. *See also* Grow
Capacity; growth; margin
calendar and, 91–93
curiosity and, 144

design for scale, 96–98, 99
doing job and, 90–91
fear of change and, 101
human side of, 89
inertia and, 101–102
management vs. leadership
mindset, 101
phases of, 98–100
self-care, 95–96
self-evaluation and, 90
skepticism and, 100
team evaluation and, 76
technology and, 88–89, 93–94
Carr, Nicolas, 13
Cathy, Truett, 195
Centers for Disease Control and
Prevention, 130
challenges. *See* quicksand
change, 139–140, 189. *See also*
Create Change; curiosity;
growth mindset; progress
accountability and, 220–221
ADHD and, 228
alignment issues and, 229
belief in agency and, 189
belief in what can be, 199
communication and, 225
described, 188–189
difficulty of, 218
fear of, 101
growth mindset and, 193–198
measuring, 221–223
obstacles to, 189
planning and, 224–225
progress and, 61
realism and, 226–227, 229
recognition and, 225–226
resources and, 229

success of efforts for, 217
tools of, 218–227
troubleshooting, 227–230
urgency and, 228
values/beliefs and, 223–224
vision and, 204
Chesky, Brian, 166
choices, 11. *See also* Smart Choices
access to, 21–22
better, 23
conscious, 23
consequences of, 2. *see also*
culture; engagement
costly, 28
impact and, 2–3
impediments to, 31
importance of, 4
rational, 24
remotely conscious, 23
routine, 28, 113
simple, 5
strategic, 22
subconscious factors in,
23–26
trivial, 27
types of, 27–28
value of, 3
wise, 2
chunking, 92
circumstances, 17. *See also* control
clarity, 58, 77–78, 109, 110, 116,
132, 227. *See also* mirror,
checking
Cloud, Henry, 229
coaches, 45–47, 49, 50–51
collaborative work, 73–74. *See also*
teams
Collins, Jim, 156

Comer, John Mark, 102
commonplace books, 147–151
communication
alignment and, 229
creating change and, 225
learning styles and, 210–212
questions to prepare for, 161
of vision, 208–212
communications, digital, 12–13,
24–25, 111–112. *See also*
quicksand
community, 42, 81–84. *See also*
relationships
compensation, 25, 61
complacency, 15, 102, 142
complexity, growing, 14. *See also*
quicksand
computers, capacity and, 88–89
confirmation bias, 25
Confront Reality, 29, 32, 36–55. *See*
also Smart Choices; truth
areas to evaluate, 40–42
BE SMART! 55, 86
challenging questions and,
44–45
checking mirror, 58–69
continuing, 53
data and, 43–44
fear and, 54
fresh eyes and, 45–53
importance of, 30
narrowing focus of, 43
overview of, 29–30
reasons for avoiding, 37–40
Review Your Crew, 11, 72–86.
see also teams
"see for yourself", 45
consultants, 45–53

control, 108
  lack of, 10, 17. *see also*
    quicksand
conversations. *See* curiosity
  conversations; talking to
  people
counsel, 49
courage, 101
  leadership and, 63–64
  purpose and, 132
Covey, Stephen, 106, 108, 139
COVID-19, 17, 94
Create Change, 33, 188–199. *See
  also* change; Smart Choices
  BE SMART! 199, 213, 230
  overview of, 31–32
  See the Unseen, 202–213. *see
    also* vision
  Sharpen Your Tools, 216–230.
    see also tools
creativity
  curiosity and, 142
  in liminal space, 107
  questions and, 159, 164–165
culture, 2, 26, 61
curiosity. *See also* change; Fuel
  Curiosity; information;
  learning
  adaptability and, 142
  barriers to, 144
  bias against, 137–138, 140
  capacity and, 144
  commonplace books, 147–151
  contagiousness of, 143
  creativity and, 142
  energy and, 142
  future and, 141

growth and, 141–142
importance of, 152–153
innovation and, 142
listening to customers,
  136–137
need for, 140–144
possibilities and, 141
questions and, 144–145
Quinn's, 136–137
reading and, 146–147
rediscovering, 144–147
relevance and, 140–141
talking to people and, 145
test and learn, 153
vitality and, 140–141
curiosity conversations, 168,
  172–173. *See also* talking to
  people
Curious Mind, A (Grazer), 172
customer reports, 2
customers, listening to, 136–
  137
cycle, virtuous, 29, 32–33

D
da Vinci, Leonardo, 147
Danziger, Shai, 26
Davis, Tchiki, 193
de Bono, Edward, 176
death, lack of sleep and, 129
decision fatigue, 26
decision overload, 26
decisions. *See* choices
decline bias, 25
delegators, 98–99, 100
Deloitte, 74
denial, living in, 38

design thinking, 145
designers, 99–100
developers, 99, 100
development, leadership, 67–69.
    See also growth
Dewey, John, 52
diet, 122, 128
differences, individual, 26
digital communications, 12–13,
    24–25, 111–112
disconnection, 39
discovery, questions for, 163–164
disengagement, 39
distractions, 13–14, 39. *See also*
    quicksand
diversity, 48, 76
doers, 98, 100
dopamine, 24
Dorsey, Jack, 166
doubt, 195, 196
drivers, key, 86
Drucker, Peter, 3, 59, 64, 91, 165,
    186
Duggin, William, 203
Dupree, Max, 36, 37
Dweck, Carol, 193

E
easy, vs. simple, 5
Edgeworth, Maria, 117
Edison, Thomas, 149
education, 26
Effective Executive, The (Drucker), 3
effectiveness, 3
ego, setting aside, 217
Einstein, Albert, 136, 156, 158
email, 12, 111–112

emergent interviewing, 124
Emerson, Ralph Waldo, 132
emotions, 23, 24
empathy, 124
energy, 16, 95–96, 102, 120–133
    assessing level of, 121
    auditing, 124–125
    curiosity and, 142
    diet and, 122, 128
    emotional/mental, 122,
        123–124
    empathy and, 124
    energy management plan,
        127–133
    exercise and, 122, 127–128
    hydration and, 128
    owning, 125–126
    purpose and, 132
    recreation and, 131
    relationships and, 122–124,
        131–132
    replenishing, 125
    sleep and, 122, 128, 129
    spiritual practices and,
        132–133
    vision and, 204–205
engagement, 2, 39, 60
environment, choices and, 26
essential, vs. urgent, 8
ethnographic interviewing, 158,
    179
exercise, 122, 127–128
exhaustion/fatigue, 16, 18, 19. *See
    also* energy; quicksand
Expand Your Energy, 96, 120–133.
    See also energy
expectations, realistic, 229–230

experience, 25, 46
exploration, questions for,
    163–164

F
failure, 38, 54
faith traditions, 26. *See also* spiritual practices
fatigue, 16, 18, 19, 128. *See also*
    energy; quicksand
fear, 16, 25
    of current reality, 54
    of failure, 38
    overcoming, 187
feedback, 47, 48, 49. *See also* Confront Reality
finances, evaluating reality of, 42
fixed mindset, 193–194, 195
focus days, 112–113
focus groups, 136
followers, 64
food insecurity, choices and, 22
Ford, Henry, 88, 190
Frames of Mind (Gardner), 210–211
Frankl, Viktor, 21, 115
Franklin, Benjamin, 120
friends, firing, 131–132
Fuel Curiosity, 33, 136–153. *See
    also* curiosity; Smart Choices
    Ask, Don't Tell, 156–169. *see
        also* questions
    BE SMART! 153, 169, 183
    overview of, 31
    relation with Grow Capacity,
        144
    Talk with Strangers, 172–183.
        see also curiosity conversations; talking to people

Fuller, Thomas, 216
futility. *See* quicksand
future. *See also* vision
    counsel and, 49
    curiosity and, 141, 142
    evaluating team and, 76
    influence over, 33
    optimism about, 62

G
Gance, Abel, 202
gap, vs. opportunity, 67
Gardner, Howard, 95, 210–211
Gates, Bill, 62
Genchi Gembutsu, 45
geography, 26
George, Bill, 45
gift, unexpected, 145
Gino, Francesca, 143
giving up, 19
goals, 3, 34, 78–79, 85–86, 221–
    223. *See also* planning;
    strategy
Godin, Seth, 197
Goldsmith, Marshall, 39
Gonzalez, Ruben, 186–187
Good to Great (Collins), 156
graphic novels, 21
Grazer, Brian, 62, 172–173
Grow Capacity, 32, 88–103. *See also*
    capacity; growth; margin;
    Smart Choices
    BE SMART! 103, 117, 133
    Expand Your Energy, 96,
        120–133. *see also* energy
    overview of, 30–31
    relation with Fuel Curiosity,
        144

Stop and Think, 95, 106–117. *see also* margin

growth, 69. *See also* capacity; change; development, leadership; progress
   committing to, 194–195
   curiosity and, 141–142
   questions and, 157

growth mindset, 190, 193–198. *See also* change; locus of control

H

habits, 28

Hadeed, Kristen, 58

Hagrid, 231

Harlem Children's Zone (HCZ), 199

Harvard Business Review, 73, 217, 225

heads-up, heads-down challenge, 109

health. *See also* energy
   evaluating reality of, 42
   sleep and, 130

Heifetz, Ronald, 109

helplessness, 10, 19, 129. *See also* quicksand

Hendricks, Howard, 152

High Performance Teams. *See* teams

Hill, Napoleon, 53

hockey, 72–73

hodgepodge book. *See* commonplace books

Holtz, Lou, 82

hope, 101

Hsieh, Tony, 165

Huffington, Arianna, 130

hurry, 102

hydration, 128

I

ideas, 47, 143, 149–150. *See also* curiosity

Iguodala, Andre, 130

immersion, 95

impact, 2–3
   curiosity and, 137
   influence over, 33
   scaling, 21–34

improvement, identifying opportunities for, 32. *See also* Confront Reality

improvement projects, 61

Indiana Jones and the Last Crusade (film), 1

inertia, 15–16, 101–102, 143

influence, Smart Choices and, 23

information. *See also* curiosity; learning
   collecting without taking action, 125
   learning styles and, 210–212
   memory and, 148
   questions and, 157
   receiving, 146–147

innovation
   curiosity and, 137, 142
   in liminal space, 107

instincts, 23

intelligences, 210–211

intentionality, 16–17. *See also* planning

interruptions, 13–14, 39. *See also* quicksand

interview questions, 165–166

interviewing, emergent, 124

interviewing, ethnographic, 158, 179

invention, capacity and, 88–89
isolation, 95
It's Your Ship (Abrashoff), 217

J
Jakes, T. D., 96, 97
Japan, 74
job, doing, 90–91
Jobs, Steve, 202

K
Katzenbach, John, 84
kedging, 127–128
knowing-doing gap, 125
knowledge workers, 91
Kodak, 140
Kotter, John, 225
Kwik, Jim, 146

L
lagniappe, 145
leaders
    developing, 99
    ego of, 217
    growing. *see* capacity; growth
    as own adversary, 17
    roles of, 81, 98–100
    serving vs. self-serving, 64
    trust in, 61
leadership
    absentee, 39
    capacity for, 89. *see also* capacity
    challenges of, 8–9. *see also*
        quicksand
    courage and, 63–64
    definitions of, 188. *see also* change
    evaluating reality of, 41. *see
        also* Confront Reality; mir-
        ror, checking; teams

fear-based, 102
leadership team. *See also* teams
    roles of, 81
    sharing vision with, 208
Leadership Without Easy Answers
    (Heifetz), 109
Leading Change (Kotter), 225
Leading Minds (Gardner), 95
learning, 31. *See also* curiosity;
        Fuel Curiosity; information
    daily, 196
    growth and, 141–142
    lifelong, 62
    sharing, 196–197
    test and learn, 145–146, 153
learning styles, 210–212
legacy
    evaluating reality of, 42
    Smart Choices and, 23
Levav, Jonathan, 26
library, 112
life, evaluating reality of, 41
limbic region, 24
liminal space, 106–107, 108. *See
    also* margin
Limitless (Kwik), 146
listening, 117, 136–137, 158–159,
    216–217
locus of control, 190–193. *See also*
    growth mindset
Lombardi, Vince, 16
loneliness, 129
longevity, curiosity and, 137

M
management mindset, 101
manager, role of, 108
Marcus Aurelius, 147
margin, 108–117

clarifying purpose and, 132
creating, 94–95, 111–115
defined, 94
learning from past and,
    110–111
in moment, 115–117
as time machine, 109–111
martial arts, 115
Marvel, 21
mastermind group, 53
Maxwell, John, 72, 75, 220
McChrystal, Stanley, 166
media, digital. *See* communica-
    tions, digital
mediocrity, 19. *See also* quicksand
Medtronic, 45
meetings, 11–12. *See also* quick-
    sand; teams
    action items in, 221
    effective, 84–85
    personal productivity and,
        92
    poorly run, 11
    successful, 11
    virtual, 94
    vision and, 84–85
memory, 148, 150
mentors, 49–50
metrics, outcome, 86
Miller, Don, 120
Miller, Larry, 140
mindset, growth, 193–198
Miracle on Ice, 72–73
mirror, checking, 58–69
    identifying strengths/
        weaknesses, 69
    owning strengths/weaknesses,
        65–66
    questions for, 59–65

mistakes, 233
    avoiding, 194
    learning from, 192–193
    others', learning from, 195–
        196
Model Ts, 88
morale, 2
motivation. *See* energy
music industry, 140–141

N
Napoleon (film), 202
Napoleon Bonaparte, 202–203
Napster, 140–141
Netflix, 140
Nohria, Nitin, 11, 108
Non-Runner's Marathon Trainer
    (Kole, Whitsett, and Dolge-
    ner), 192
normalcy, idealizing, 108
notebooks, 147. *See also* common-
    place books
notes. *See also* commonplace
    books
    during conversations, 180
    reviewing, 150–151
Nouwen, Henri, 8

O
omission bias, 25
opportunity, 4, 22, 67
optimism, 39–40, 62–63, 226
organizations
    ADHD in, 228
    evaluating reality of, 41
    life cycles of, 140
    organic, 100
outsiders, confronting reality
    and, 45–53

P

pandemic, 17, 94
passion, 209, 220
past
    feedback and, 49
    learning from, 110–111
Patton, George, 16
peer groups, 53
peer pressure, 26
peers, assessment of leadership
    and, 64
people of color, 22
perfection, 146
performance
    vs. appearance, 39
    metrics of, 86
    peers' assessment of, 64
    supervisor's assessment of,
        65
    teams and, 74
performance improvement
    goals and, 79
    meetings and, 84–85
performance plateau, 31
perspective, 109, 110
pessimism, 62–63, 100, 226
Pfeffer, Jeffrey, 125
pillow book. *See* commonplace
    books
planning, 16–17, 224–225. *See also*
    strategy
    questions for, 161–162
plans, development, 67–69
Plato, 198
point of diminishing returns, 28
Porter, Michael, 11, 108
positives, false, 66
possibilities, curiosity and, 141

potential, 18, 89. *See also* capacity;
    vision
    engagement and, 60
    evaluating team and, 76
    lost, 99–100
Potter, Harry, 231
poverty, choices and, 22
power, true, 4
pressure, sustained, 96
priorities, goals and, 78–79
problem-solving, 52, 159–
    160, 162–163. *See also*
    brainstorming
productivity, personal, 91–93. *See
    also* capacity
profits, 2
progress, 189. *See also* change;
    growth
    celebrating, 198
    change and, 61
    identifying actions to take for,
        192
    tracking, 69
project, selecting, 191
purpose, 77, 195
    clarity of, 77–78, 132
    courage and, 132
    energy and, 132

Q

quality, 74
questions, 138, 156. *See also*
    curiosity
    applications of, 161–166
    better, 144–145, 166–167
    challenging, 44–45, 47
    creativity and, 159, 164–165
    curiosity and, 144–145

for curiosity conversations/
talking to strangers, 168,
178–180
for discovery, 163–164
importance of, 157–160
information and, 157
for interviews, 165–166
leading, 167
number of, 145, 156–157
open vs. closed, 166
other people's, 166
preparing communications
and, 161
prioritizing, 179
problem-solving and, 159–160,
162–163
questions created by, 158–159
recipients of, 157
right, 46, 59–65
for self, 168
single-barrel, 167
for strategy/planning, 161–
162
for team, 168
transport, 158
question-to-statement ratio, 156
quicksand, 20, 189, 218
characteristics of, 10
elements of, 11–14. *see also*
distractions; meetings
escaping, 19. *see also* Smart
Choices
fighting, 10
identifying, 14–17, 20
leader's response to, 18–20
learning to lead in, 18
learning to swim in, 10–11
Quinn, Fergal, 136–137

R
racial injustices, 22
rapid prototyping, 146
reading, 146–147
realism, 226–227, 229
reality. *See also* Confront Reality;
truth
fear of, 54
importance of, 29
reasons for avoiding, 37–40
recognition, 63, 225–226
recreation, 131
reinvention, 60–61
relationships. *See also* community
energy and, 122–124, 131–132
evaluating reality of, 41
valuing, 61
relevance
curiosity and, 138, 140–141
questions and, 160
resource allocation, 79, 229
response, 115–116
responsibility, vs. blame, 63
results, 61, 64
retreats, personal, 114
review, daily, 113–114
Review Your Crew, 11, 72–86. *See
also* teams
rewards, desire for, 24–25
rhythm of life, 95
Richardson-Heron, Dara, 165
risks, small, 197–198
rituals, morning, 113
Rohr, Richard, 108
roles, 67, 80–81, 108. *See also*
activity
Ruthless Elimination of Hurry, The
(Comer), 102

S

sales, 2
Santayana, George, 110
Sawatsky, John, 144
scale, design for, 96–98
scorecards, 85–86, 221–223
Secret, The (Miller and Blanchard), 109
Secret of Teams, The (Miller), 75
Secrets of CEOs, The (Tappin), 126
"see for yourself", 45
See the Unseen, 202–213. *See also* vision
seeing. *See* vision
Sei Shonagon, 147
self, evaluation of, 58–69. *See also* mirror, checking
self-care, 95–96. *See also* energy
selfishness, 64
self-serving bias, 25
Seneca, 147
servant leadership, 64
Seven Kinds of Smart (Armstrong), 211–212
7 Habits of Highly Effective People, The (Covey), 139
Shackleton, Ernest, 62
Shakespeare, William, 16
Shallows, The (Carr), 13
Sharpen Your Tools, 216–230. *See also* tools
Shiv, Baba, 24
short-term thinking, 39
simple, vs. easy, 5
Sinek, Simon, 24, 195
sleep, 122, 128, 129
Sleep Revolution, The (Huffington), 130
Smart Choices, 27. *See also* Confront Reality; Create Change; Fuel Curiosity; Grow Capacity
    acting on, 218. *see also* tools
    collective potential of, 6, 29, 32–33, 144
    described, 23, 28
    goals and, 34
    interconnectedness of, 89
    operationalizing, 4
    overview of, 28–32
social media, 12, 13, 24–25. *See also* communications, digital
socioeconomic factors, choices and, 22, 26
Socrates, 36–37, 58
Southwest Airlines, 204
specificity, in plans, 68
spiritual practices, 42, 132–133. *See also* faith traditions
stamina. *See* energy
Star Wars (film), 189–190
starting point, 30, 32. *See also* Confront Reality
status quo, 189. *See also* quicksand
Stop and Think, 95, 106–117. *See also* margin
story, power to write. *See* energy
Strategic Intuition (Duggin), 203
strategy. *See also* goals; planning
    goals and, 3, 79
    questions for, 161–162
    vision and, 205–206
strengths, 32, 65–66, 69. *See also* Confront Reality
structure, 79, 96–98
Student Maid, 58

success, 15, 31, 38, 140
success criteria, 64
superheroes, 21
superpowers, 21
supervisor, assessment of leadership and, 65
Sutton, Robert, 125
Swatsky, Jeff, 167
switching costs, 92–93

T
Talk with Strangers, 145, 172–183. *See also* curiosity conversations; talking to people
talking to people. *See also* curiosity conversations
  applying lessons from, 181–182
  choosing people to talk to, 173–175
  curiosity and, 145
  follow up, 182–183
  gaining audience, 175–177
  going off script, 177–178
  maximizing conversation, 177–180
  objective in, 178
  preparation for, 177, 178
  processing conversation, 181
  questions for, 178–180
  sharing experience of, 182
  taking notes, 180
Tappin, Steve, 126
tasks, 91–93, 103
teams, 73–74. *See also* leadership team; meetings
  community and, 81–84
  diversity on, 76
  effective meetings and, 84–85

  evaluating, 41, 75–86
  good vs. outstanding, 82
  High Performance Team Assessment, 86
  improving, 75
  job of, 90
  performance and, 74
  questions for, 168
  role clarity in, 80–81
  scorecards for, 85–86
  sense of purpose, 77
  shared goals and, 78–79
  types of, 81
technology, capacity and, 88–89
test and learn, 145–146, 153
texts. *See* communications, digital
theta waves, 149
thinking, changing, 191
Thousand Miles in a Million Years, A (Miller), 120
threshold, 106, 107. *See also* margin
time, 91–93. *See also* calendar; margin
tools, 218–227. *See also* communication; vision
  accountability, 220–221
  communication, 225
  measurement, 221–223
  passion, 220
  planning, 224–225
  recognition, 225–226
  values/beliefs, 223–224
  vision, 227
total quality management, 74
Toynbee, Arnold, 140
Toyota, 45
tracking, 69, 93

troubleshooting, 227
trust, in leader, 61
truth, 29. *See also* Confront Reality; reality
   avoiding, 37
   from outsiders, 47
Twain, Mark, 172
typing vs. writing, 150

U
Unmistakable Creative Podcast, 197
urgency, 26, 228
urgent, vs. essential, 8
user, in design, 145

V
value, adding, 3
   to personal board members, 49
   serving and, 64
values/beliefs, 223–224
   articulating, 24
   choices and, 24
   living, 61–62
   personal experience and, 46
   spiritual practices, 42, 132–133
viewpoints, outside, 45–53
vision, 59–60, 102, 203–213, 220
   buy-in and, 205
   communicating, 208–212
   direction and, 204
   energy and, 204–205
   finding, 206–208
   focus and, 205
   for future, 108

   importance of, 203–206
   meetings and, 84–85
   Napoleon's, 202–203
   need for clarity in, 227
   need for planning in, 224
   positive change and, 204
   strategy and, 205–206
   timeline for, 206
vitality, curiosity and, 138, 140–141
von Oech, Roger, 137

W
Waiting for Superman (film), 199
"Walden" (Emerson), 132
Ward, William, 226
weaknesses, 65–66, 67, 69
Weiner, Jeff, 166
Welch, Jack, 166, 209
Welch, Suzy, 166
well-roundedness, 65–66
Whack on the Side of the Head, A (von Oech), 137
white water, perpetual, 139
"why", 195, 212. *See also* purpose; vision
Win Every Day (Miller), 222
Wisdom of Teams, The (Katzenbach), 84
Wooden, John, 60–61
work, approach to, 175
writing vs. typing, 150

Z
zibaldone. See commonplace books

ABOUT THE AUTHOR

Mark Miller is a business leader, best-selling author, and communicator.

Mark started his Chick-fil-A career working as an hourly team member in 1977. In 1978, he joined the corporate staff working in the warehouse and mailroom. Since that time, he has provided leadership for corporate communications, field operations, quality and customer satisfaction, training and development, leadership development, and more. During his tenure with Chick-fil-A, the company has grown from seventy-five restaurants to over 2,700 locations with annual sales exceeding $17 billion.

He began writing almost twenty years ago when he teamed up with Ken Blanchard, coauthor of *The One Minute Manager*, to write *The Secret: What Great Leaders Know and Do*. The book you now hold in your hand is his tenth. With over one million books in print in more than twenty-five languages, Mark's global impact continues to grow.

In addition to his writing, Mark enjoys encouraging and equipping leaders. Over the years, he's traveled to dozens of countries teaching for numerous international organizations.

Mark is also an avid photographer who loves shooting in some of the most remote places on the planet. Past adventures have taken him to the jungles of Rwanda in search of silverback gorillas, across Drake's passage to Antarctica, and to several high-altitude destinations including Everest Base Camp.

Married to Donna, his high school sweetheart, for almost forty years, they have two sons, Justin and David, a daughter-in-law, Lindsay, and three amazing grandchildren, Addie, Logan, and Finn.

Mark would love to connect with you via the following:

Web: **MarkMillerLeadership.com**
Instagram: **MarkMillerLeadership**
Twitter: **MarkMillerLeads**
Linkedin: **Mark Miller**
Cell: **678-612-8441**